THE GOLDEN AGE
OF ROMAN BRITAIN

Guy de la Bédoyère

TEMPUS

First published 1999

PUBLISHED IN THE UNITED KINGDOM BY:

Tempus Publishing Ltd
The Mill, Brimscombe Port
Stroud, Gloucestershire GL5 2QG

PUBLISHED IN THE UNITED STATES OF AMERICA BY:

Tempus Publishing Inc.
2A Cumberland Street
Charleston, SC 29401

Tempus books are available in France, Germany and Belgium
from the following addresses:

Tempus Publishing Group
21 Avenue de la République
37300 Joué-lès-Tours
FRANCE

Tempus Publishing Group
Gustav-Adolf-Straße 3
99084 Erfurt
GERMANY

Tempus Publishing Group
Place de L'Alma 4/5
1200 Brussels
BELGIUM

British Library Cataloguing in Publication Data.
A catalogue record for this book is available from the British Library.

ISBN 0 7524 1417 8

Typesetting and origination by Tempus Publishing.
PRINTED AND BOUND IN GREAT BRITAIN.

Contents

The illustrations

Text figures

The cover illustration shows coins from the Hoxne Hoard. (Courtesy of the Trustees of the British Museum.)

Foreword

The character of any period or time in human history is often largely defined by the works, influence, and tastes of its ruling class. For example, ancient Egypt is a civilisation perceived principally through the burial habits and religious relics of its pharaohs. In the same way Tudor England is, for us, the world of Henry VIII and Elizabeth I and their court circles. The joint monarchs, William and Mary, have given their names to a whole class of art and architecture which they patronised. Of course it is invariably the case that this ignores the vast majority of the population, for whom life has been eternal thankless labour. That, however, is the point. Without the defining, fashion-setting, tastes of the elite many periods would be indistinguishable from one another.

In recent studies of Roman Britain the great country villas have taken second place to the profuse native farmsteads, and in particular those which can be associated with the villa estates. Relatively few villas have been the subject of comprehensive modern excavation and even fewer are visible today. But as the main phenomenon of the fourth century in Roman Britain they are, as has long been accepted, the result of the existence of an extremely wealthy elite. The lavishness of the villa facilities and decorations show that their owners dominated the luxury market, patronised and funded the existence of a high-quality artisan class. They also dominated the social and economic structures within which many of the ordinary rural population spent their lives.

In other words the owners of the fourth-century villas define their age for us. Through their mosaics, wall-paintings, architecture, and possessions we can understand some of how they perceived and experienced their world. This book is an attempt to trace the fourth century in Roman Britain and to place the remains of houses like Bignor and Woodchester, and treasures like Thetford and Hoxne, in an historical, literary, and social context. There are all sorts of questions that can be asked. For example, is the classical imagery so widely used in the iconography and art of the period evidence of an educated and sophisticated culture? Or was elite Romano-British society simply trying to present itself to the rest of the world as a part of classical society? Inevitably there are so many pieces of the puzzle missing that much can only be guessed at. But the fourth century is often presented as a kind of preamble to the end of the Roman period in Britain; this was not, and cannot have been, how it was perceived at the time and it is from that perspective that we need to look at what can only be described as Roman Britain's Golden Age.

The opportunity has been taken to use some ancient sources which are not widely known amongst students of Roman Britain, especially the letters of Sidonius but also material from other writers like Augustine and Jerome. They help make good the very limited amount of material directly relevant to Roman Britain which survives and undoubtedly help place this remote province in a greater context. I hope that these will help encourage wider reading and to develop a more imaginative synthesis of Romano-British history and archaeology.

I would like to thank Peter Kemmis Betty for his enthusiastic reception of the book, and for his many useful comments, as well as Andrew Burnett, Stephen Johnson, Richard Reece, and Roger Tomlin for their comments on my paper on Carausius and Virgil which led directly to this book. I am also extremely grateful to Catherine Johns of the British Museum who has done so much work on the great treasure hoards of Roman Britain for her invaluable help and advice. Thanks for help with illustrations are due to Keith Lowe of the Department of Prehistoric and Romano-British Antiquities, Janet Larkin of the Department of Coins and Medals, both of the British Museum, and also Brenda Compton (Bignor villa) and N.J. Carr (Brading villa).

1   *Roman Britain in the fourth century showing principal sites and locations mentioned in the text. See also* **10** *for the other forts of the Saxon Shore.*

1 Introduction

When Constantine the Great was proclaimed emperor at York in 306 much of Britain had been Roman for more than 250 years. The process had been slow, with the military conquest of the north in particular having stretched over generations. Despite this, and despite the fact that northern Britain was made up of areas which remained outside Roman control or which were heavily garrisoned, much of the rest of Britain had become steadily romanized. In 306 a century lay ahead in which Roman Britain came closest to being a true part of the classical world. All the abstract classical forms and concepts of towns and administrative systems, characteristics of romanization, had been imposed in varying degrees. But, until the end of the third century, she had remained a peripheral and mysterious part of the Empire.

Stimulation for much of what was so remarkable about the fourth century in Roman Britain came from the classical world of Greek and Roman civilisation. Very rich families were fairly widespread across the Empire at this time. They owned huge tracts of land and often enjoyed political status in more than one province. Their wealth allowed indulgence in luxury goods from across the Empire and they took pleasure in all aspects of classical culture.

In the early second century the Roman historian Florus described Britain as being of no intrinsic value to the Empire, but whose possession was essential 'to the bearing of imperial power'. In other words Britain was perceived as practically and culturally marginal, but the sheer bloody-mindedness of its inhabitants and its remoteness made it a trophy. In the fourth century Britain was unusual for different reasons. She had been largely insulated from the barbarian incursions of the third century and, perhaps more importantly, also from the worst of the internal wars between would-be emperors. This made her natural fertility and temperate climate all the more advantageous. Any sense of cultural inferiority was replaced with a new self-confidence though, in the rest of the Roman world, the Romano-British were regarded as ignorant and uncultivated bumpkins.

The eighteenth- and nineteenth-century antiquarians who excavated some of Roman Britain's greatest monuments had no qualms about indulging their imaginations (**2, plate 1**). This often led to colourful interpretations — buildings showing traces of fire were generally believed to have been destroyed in an explosion of barbarian vandalism and murderous hatred of the Romans — but at least they enjoyed themselves. Men such as Samuel Lysons had one huge advantage over their modern counterparts: their education was dominated by classical languages, history, and mythology. This placed them much closer to the mind-set of the people whose remains they were uncovering. Modern preoccupations with 'models' and statistics have led to some scientific rigour but also diverted attention from the art and imagination of Roman Britain.

2   *The fourth-century Medusa floor from the villa at Bignor (West Sussex), as recorded by Samuel Lysons in 1817. (Copyright — The British Museum).*

The bulk of the evidence for Romano-British culture, in the form of thought, literature, and music, does not and cannot survive. So, it is easy to behave as if they never existed. But the discovery of several major treasure hoards in the last few decades has shown that, during the fourth century in Roman Britain, intellectual and artistic life had become more sophisticated than is sometimes appreciated.

Our central problem is the nature of the written evidence for events in Roman Britain. For the first and second centuries we are reasonably well off with Tacitus and Dio Cassius dominating the surviving texts. The addition of epigraphic evidence in the form of monumental stone inscriptions and military diplomas provides invaluable details about military dispositions, the names of governors, and building activity. Apart from a peak in military inscription production in the early third century thereafter the material steadily becomes a great deal more scattered and unreliable though occasional chinks of light appear in the form of sources such as Ammianus Marcellinus. Regardless of their other shortcomings all these sources share one common problem: they are exclusively external. We have no extant histories written in Roman Britain, or by the Romano-British. What does exist is of diverse quality and many events or individuals are known only from single sentences. Tacitus, who supplies the greatest detail about military campaigns, was writing about an island he had never visited and using secondhand documents and inaccurate maps.

Much of what happened in the third and fourth centuries in Britain is a mystery. The fragmentation of the Empire and rule by a multiplicity of legitimate emperors, the episodic appearance of usurpers, and the tantalizingly disordered literary sources, reveal a mesmerizing array of names and reigns, many of whom and much of which had little relevance to Britain. Beyond these we are reliant on parallels from other periods and places

*3   Mid-second-century samian Form 37 bowl in the distinctive style of the prolific potter
Cinnamus of Lezoux. Such identifiable bowls have played an important role in helping date
events in Britain in the second century. From Plaxtol (Kent).*

and of course it is impossible to know whether the parallels have any relevance. The letters
of Pliny, for example, supply some of the most vivid references to villa and social life, but
he was writing at the beginning of the second century in Italy. His references to law,
society, and religion are compelling but may have nothing to do with Roman Britain.

The only alternative is archaeology but it is important to appreciate that the nature of
the evidence is that it cannot make good gaps in the history. It is the surviving history of
the first and second centuries which has made the archaeological evidence of the period
so valuable. In providing a well-established chronology it becomes possible to associate
the products of, for example, Gaulish samian potters with reasonably well-defined periods
on major military sites (**3**). Hadrian's Wall is undoubtedly the best example. As it is known
to have been built not before about 122 it is therefore self-evident that pottery and other
goods found in its primary levels must have been in circulation at that time. Armed with
this information the same products of those potters found on mundane sites like early
villas or villages make it possible for archaeologists to build up a picture of the developing
province and what was available to who and where. In this way archaeology augments,
illustrates and defines the history.

Pottery, however, like much archaeological evidence is not straightforward. Many styles
of more basic kitchen wares are far more difficult to associate with tightly-dated periods.
Coins had a tendency to circulate for years after they were issued and to be hoarded for
even longer especially if they were made of a purer silver than later became current. By

the third century these two staples become even less precise dating tools for the period. Epigraphic evidence, never common in Britain, fades away during the later third century and becomes almost exclusively confined to milestones or roadside honorific pillars. Even those are dead in the water after 337.

The most conspicuous features of fourth-century Roman Britain are the great villas and their internal decorations, principally the mosaics, and the major treasure hoards like Thetford and Hoxne. But few of these can ever be exactly dated. The collapse of coin supply by the early fifth century means that even hoards with coins of these years might in reality have been buried decades later. Pieces of silver like the Great Dish from the Mildenhall Treasure (**54, plate 11**) are almost invariably unique, which means estimating a date on subjective stylistic grounds and sidestepping the possibility that they might have been 'antiques' when buried. The net effect is that we are dealing with items which can only be attributed usually to periods covering decades. Worse, there is no Romano-British individual in this or any other period for whom a home, possessions, land, position, and income can all be identified.

Perhaps this is why later Romano-British history is often presented as a period of inevitable decline, manifested in the collapse of authority and a superficially-romanized culture in Britain. After all, the only thing we know for absolute certain is that it came to an end. Therefore we automatically seek out its causes, just as history books produced after 1945 sought in earnest to understand the causes of the Second World War. But no society operates on assumptions of its own mortality so why should this be true of the Romano-British? Sometimes Romano-British culture appears as if it was historically static, despite the routine trotting out of the progression of conquest. There is often a sense that Britain eventually found an identity in a crude provincial synthesis of the classical and 'Celtic', and then meandered through the next 300-odd years until severed from Rome. So fragile was this romanization that the moment the cultural, financial and emotional subsidy fed in by the Empire ceased it was inevitable that Britain would revert to type.

It was never like that. The Roman Britain of the fourth century would still have been identifiably Roman to any Roman from any time. The most powerful people in Britain saw themselves and their island province as a haven of classical culture. Far from a perpetual struggle to throw off the Roman yoke Britain was a safer place, insulated from the worst of the decay, the civil wars and barbarian incursions which spread across the contiguous provinces of the mainland Empire. There was a cultural revolution as the wealthy found themselves able to develop a distinctive rural lifestyle based on the possession of immense estates, and the patronage of artisans.

This is no exaggeration. The contrast in the rural landscape between the early fourth century and the century before was the appearance of substantial and elaborate country houses, almost invariably in the form of aggrandisements to existing houses. This by no means occurred at all villas but the phenomenon is detectable in almost all parts of the province which enjoyed superior agricultural land. Houses in the countryside with mosaic floors and painted wall-plaster were scarcely known in the first century. In the second they were rarer than comparable houses in towns like Verulamium. By the fourth century the reverse was true. Even modest houses exhibited a desire on the part of their owners to aspire to higher living. This lifestyle was partly characterized by a self-conscious pagan revival; traditional cults were perceived as the natural repository of Roman values and a symbolic statement of a desire to cling on to the old ways. Just as the eyes rolled-heavenward on the coins of the fourth-century emperors differ from the brutal realism of the portraits on those of their first-century predecessors, so the character of late Roman Britain was diametrically different from the pioneer days of the first century.

Early Roman Britain

Long before, but within two generations of the invasion, southern Britain was overwhelmed by the establishment of towns, trading posts, ports, and the building of roads. The Thames at London was transformed from a liquid tribal frontier into a communications hub and a commercial explosion. Her north bank creaked under the weight of wharves and warehouses while the burgeoning town unrolled from the bridgehead. Through all such towns and ports came and went the unceasing military and commercial traffic of people and supplies. It was inevitable that the city would become the capital of the new province. Trade lubricated romanization and the infrastructure to make its proliferation possible was fundamental to development.

In the countryside the tribal Britons of the south had no choice but to accept change. There is little suggestion of sustained resistance, in spite of the Revolt of Boudica in 60–1. Her opposition to Rome was entirely understandable in a political and social sense because everything she stood for was challenged by the new system. The catastrophic humiliation, embezzlement and abuse she and her people suffered led to the Revolt.

However, the reality was that Boudica wanted to preserve a social system and hierarchy which excluded the vast bulk of the population from access to trade, secure property ownership and the chance to accumulate wealth. The Empire recognized, as Tacitus so cynically observed, that the availability of the attractions and comforts of romanization were the means by which people became enslaved to the Empire. But if that was true the Britons were, for the most part, willingly enslaved. Anyone disputing that analysis might care to ask how willingly he or she would give up comforts which have only been available to the majority of the British population since the 1950s. There is no evidence of resistance to romanization in southern Britain once the Revolt had been suppressed. This of course is not evidence that there was no resistance but the general proliferation of Roman goods in most southern rural areas over succeeding decades makes it unlikely that it amounted to more than nostalgic grumbling over a samian cup filled with imported wine.

The inter-tribal wars of the pre-Roman era were outlawed and the Britons were obliged to find political identities in the names and bodies of the tribal districts (or cantons). The new district capitals (known as civitas capitals) replaced traditional tribal centres. From them the tribal zones were individually governed, but not exclusively by imported Roman administrators. Instead the old tribal hierarchies were mimicked by translation into Roman urban offices and membership of the cantonal councils. Property qualification for membership of a council was guaranteed by allowing the tribal elite to retain their lands. They thus formed the basis of the decurial class, those qualified to serve on town councils and to hold magistracies. The new towns and public buildings were partly funded by taxes

4   Late-second, early-third-century mosaic from a house at Verulamium (IV.8).

and by levying charges for admission to public office. Thus we find at Wroxeter the *civitas Cornoviorum* (the 'community of the Cornovii'), responsible for the construction of the forum in 129–30 under Hadrian. Gradually houses were built and by the late second to early third century many had mosaics and other refinements (**4**).

Beyond these obligations to Roman rule, the Britons were left to pursue their rural lives but towns promised novelties, markets, and recourse to justice. The latter is largely theoretical but occasional traces survive. A wooden writing tablet from London, dated to March 118, records a legal document involving a claim to property by one Lucius Julius Bellicus. His concern was a wood called *Verlucionium* in the cantonal area of the Cantiaci, approximating to modern Kent. This is interesting for two reasons. Firstly, we can see how a piece of land and its ownership was subject to the law and was apparently worthy of attention in the provincial capital. Secondly, the document apparently included precise details of where the land was. This shows us that the land had been surveyed and demarcated in a form which was permanent.

For ordinary people Roman government and the rule of law may have brought an improvement in personal liberty, compared to their former status in tribal hierarchies. Educated as we are to despise imperialism as an intolerable exercise in depriving people of their freedom, we forget that modern colonialism was partly driven by, or at any rate justified by, religious totalitarianism. In the Roman world the motives were different. They included the cynical exploitation of new territories, and the management of taxation but there was a different sense that being ruled by Rome necessarily meant excising features of conquered societies. Roman society genuinely believed in its beneficent features and that other people would appreciate them if given half a chance. This attitude was undoubtedly shared by British imperialists but the limitations of operating Roman power meant that there was no choice but to accommodate and integrate existing social systems rather than obliterating them.

Local cults, laws, and customs were left intact unless they involved human sacrifice or rejection of imperial authority. For the aristocracy this meant maintaining social supremacy by being educated as Romans and aping Roman ways. This might have been part of their enslavement but it laid the foundations for the fourth century by establishing an association between elitism, civilisation and Roman culture. For farming people in the south tribal wars gave way to long-term peace. Some Romans abused their position by corrupt tax-collecting and requisitioning land but these were largely corrected in the reforms after the Boudican Revolt. Under the Roman system many ordinary Britons may have welcomed the stability and access to markets. By the year 85 no-one under the age of forty-five, and that means the majority of the population, would have had any recollection of Britain without a Roman presence.

The proof is in the ground. Gaulish fine-ware bowls were used as grave goods, and right-angled stone houses replaced wattle-and-daub round houses. It is obvious that directly, or indirectly, large areas of what we call England were assimilated with the urbanized Roman world. By about 100 the northern frontier had been roughly stabilized in a zone between the Tyne and the Solway Firth. In spite of the subsequent construction of Hadrian's Wall, and the short-lived Antonine Wall, this was where Roman Britain ended and the barbarian north began. The history of the second century in Roman Britain is often seem primarily as the process of consolidating and experimenting with the northern frontier. But, however much can be made of the various crises of the northern frontier, and the strategic and tactical response of the Roman military command, the rest of Roman Britain remained on a steady and largely-undisturbed path of romanization.

Imperial prestige went into steady decline from the reign of Commodus (180–92), accelerating erosion of centralized control. His murder led to civil war. From this emerged Septimius Severus, an African, whose victory symbolized the religious and psychological swing to the East. The western half of the Empire was less sophisticated, while awareness of its insecure northern frontiers made it an onerous burden. Britain's status and identity had always been bound up with her disproportionately-large garrison and episodic border warfare. That Clodius Albinus, governor of Britain, one of the chief protagonists in the civil war surrounding the accession of Severus, could use his garrison to make a serious bid for the purple showed how dangerous Britain could be.

To prevent future governors of Britain becoming a threat, the province was divided by Septimius Severus into two: *Inferior* (north) and *Superior* (south). With two governors the garrison was split. The governor of *Inferior* was probably subordinate to the governor of *Superior*, though in some respects Britain will have still functioned as a single province. But *Inferior*, the military zone, has provided far more in the way of dating evidence thanks to the Roman army's love of inscriptions; consequently we know more governors of the north than the south in the early third century though the majority are known just as names on inscriptions.

Provoked by rebellion in northern Britain, or deciding to use it as a pretext, Septimius Severus took the opportunity to involve his sons, Caracalla and Geta, believing that a campaign would harden them up and remove them from decadent activities in Rome. The expedition was indecisive, not least because Caracalla abandoned it once his father was dead, illustrating Britain's marginal importance to the Empire in the first decade of the third century. Nevertheless, it reinforced an image of Britain, more than 150 years after Claudius invaded, as an island of extraordinary contrasts. In the south there was an urbanized Roman world, identifiable to anyone from across the Roman Empire as part of the civilized world. In the north Britain was still terrifyingly unpredictable and remote, a place where imperial reputations could be won or lost. The holding of Britain was still, therefore, something of a vanity.

The army of the north-western provinces, a very substantial force strung out along the Rhine and in Britain, was developing a local identity and loyalty. Clodius Albinus had already shown how potent this could be. In the early Empire auxiliary army units were stationed away from their provinces or regions of origin. By the third century the Empire had become so relatively static that many of these auxiliary units were drawing recruits from the sons of their soldiers, borne by local women. Ethnically and geographically the units had more in common with the provinces in which they were stationed than with their nominal homelands. Not unnaturally they were inclined to support a usurper from amongst their leaders, especially if he had proved his qualities in the field. Britain's garrison became a willing party to this process of fragmentation.

The short-lived Severan dynasty ended as violently as it had begun. A brief succession of members of Severus' family ended with the murder of Severus Alexander in 235 by soldiers who resented his attempts to bribe German tribes not to attack the Empire. Alexander was succeeded by Maximinus I, who started at the bottom of the army and rose to become a legionary commander and a provincial governor. In 238 he too was murdered. For much of the rest of the third century, until the accession of Diocletian in 284, there was a series of short-lived emperors who enjoyed very different degrees of control over the imperial provinces.

Britain ceased to be of any great significance to Roman historians, and is rarely mentioned after 211. Traditionally she only became important when a great campaign was undertaken, or when a war broke out. Many military inscriptions from the first half of the third century record a sustained effort to assert loyalty to the incumbent regime, restore army buildings and facilities, probably to keep troops busy. For example, at Vindolanda in 223 a gate was restored, and at Lanchester the baths, the headquarters building, and the armouries were all rebuilt between 238–44. In this way Britain's military infrastructure was maintained, and even expanded.

Around the same time a seaborne threat led to the construction of two new forts much further south. The design used at Brancaster (Norfolk) and Reculver (Kent) (**10**) belongs to the second-century tradition of a rampart-backed stone wall, curved corners, and internal towers. The approximate date is confirmed by an early third-century inscription from Reculver which records the dedication of a shrine in the headquarters building and its hall. The new forts symbolize a crucial change in Britain. Until the early third century the military history of Britain was dominated by the northern frontier. Over the next

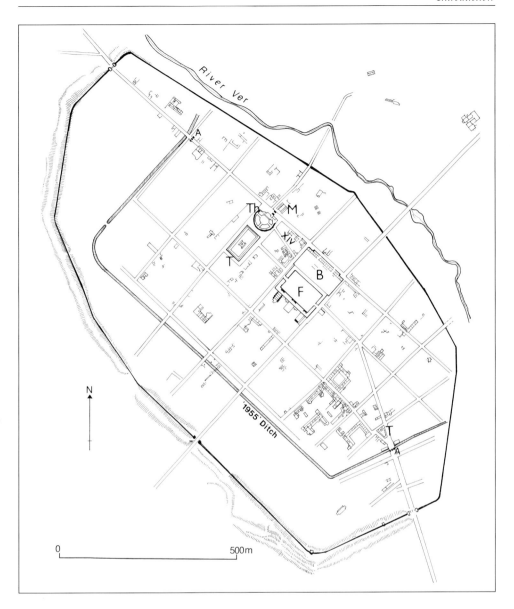

5   Plan of Verulamium *(St Albans). The third-century walls enclosed a town whose infrastructure was mostly in place by the second century: basilica (B), forum (F), temples (T), theatre (Th), and market (M). (After Niblett).*

hundred years it took second place to the development of the shore defences of the south and east. By the beginning of the fourth century some of the older military installations, especially on the northern frontier, had decayed to the point of ruin. This was in spite of the rebuilding work recorded in the north in the early 200s. Britain was becoming, if not isolated, at least distanced from the Empire as a whole.

The men sent to govern Britain's two new provinces were of minimal imperial significance and practically nothing is known about any of the names testified on inscriptions. Britain's administrative infrastructure was technically in place and urban romanization had been a fact of life for generations. Meanwhile, Caracalla's grant of universal citizenship in 212 at one stroke elevated most of the Romano-British to a status which was itself instantly devalued by being made ubiquitous.

The civilian part of the province has less in the way of datable evidence. This is always the case for Roman Britain, regardless of the period. Datable inscriptions are largely from military sites in the north and therefore record the activities of military units. Most epigraphic evidence for civilians is on undated tombstones or altars. These are nearly all from towns or the extra-mural settlements in the military north. Verulamium (St Albans), is a good example of a major Romano-British town known to have had most urban facilities such as forum and basilica, theatre, walls (recently-finished or in progress), industries, temples, and a substantial number of well-appointed townhouses (**5**). Here, and at other towns, the main public building programmes were effectively complete. Yet we know practically nothing about the urban population. Not a single tombstone or memorial of the tens of thousands of people who once lived here has survived in legible form.

Most public-building development can be pinned down to the years between 75 and 160, at least in those cases where inscriptions survive, like the Hadrianic example at Wroxeter, or where archaeology has given an approximate date. However, Britain has produced little evidence for 'civic munificence'. Elsewhere in the Empire wealthy local people often bought community popularity and status through the gift or endowment of public facilities. The forum inscriptions from Verulamium and Wroxeter suggest that in Britain imperial initiative was needed and that involvement by the wealthy was collective rather than individual.

Almost alone amongst the usually-anonymous Romano-British urban worthies is Marcus Aurelius Lunaris. His name indicates that citizenship was probably acquired by his father or grandfather during the reign of Aurelius (161–80). In the year 237 Lunaris was a *sevir Augustalis* (priest) of Augustus at York and Lincoln, and was involved in trading goods in and out of Bordeaux. There he set up an altar, thanking the goddess 'Boudig' for her protection. It has the additional value of recording that both York and Lincoln were in *Britannia Inferior* (**6**).

Lucius Viducius Placidus came from near Rouen (*Rotomagus*) in Gaul. At the mouth of the Scheldt in Holland he left an altar dedicated to the goddess Nehalennia. He also dedicated an arch and gate at York in 221 to Neptune(?), the Genius of the Place and the Spirits of the Emperors. Placidus calls himself a trader (*negotiator*) and was probably dealing in goods transported across the North Sea between Holland and eastern Britain, a pattern reflected in the distribution of some imported pottery. The inscription from York is incomplete but, like Lunaris, he may have added that he was a priest. If so, that would reflect the traditional association of wealth with civic and public religious responsibilities in the Roman world. Another altar, of similar date, from the mouth of the Scheldt, and also dedicated to Nehalennia, records the name of Marcus Secund(inius) Silvanus, a trader in pottery (*negotiator cretarius*) with Britain.

6   *Altar erected by Marcus*
    Aurelius Lunaris at
    Bordeaux. His name is
    visible in the second line.
    The names of York
    (Eboracum) *and Lincoln*
    (Lindum) *appear in the*
    third and fourth lines
    respectively. AD 237.

Lunaris, Placidus, and Silvanus were Roman merchants who moved goods, men, and money between provinces. Importantly, their connections were all with northern Britain, *Britannia Inferior*. This was the military area of Britain, and therefore their trading profits may well have been dominated by sales to the army. They had status in different provinces and used some of their profits to express their gratitude, not only in religious dedications, but in practical contributions to the towns where they made their money. None of the three was a man of great significance though they were clearly influential men of their time and place. It seems extremely unlikely that they were especially unusual and that therefore their prominence in the record is simply due to the fact that evidence for others like them has generally not survived or was not produced. Certainly there is nothing like this from after the early third century.

From the days of the conquest through to the end of the second century the fine-ware trade in western Europe had been monopolized by the Gaulish samian industries. Their gaudy orange-red vessels circulated in phenomenal quantities, particularly in the late first century (**3**). Distinctive styles, and the use of name-stamps, makes it as described above a very valuable dating tool. Samian turns up at practically every site of Roman date until the early years of the third century. From then on samian dwindled steadily both in quantity and quality until it disappeared altogether by about 250.

7   *Mortarium signed by Sennianus of* Durobrivae *(Water Newton). The signature is exceptional. Late second or third century.*

The Romano-British fine-ware market was thereafter filled mainly by indigenous pottery industries, such as the Oxfordshire area and the Nene Valley in Cambridgeshire. Most had existed before the fall of the samian industries, but the latter's collapse gave them the opportunity to expand. Although their products are individual the potters rarely marked their names on the wares or used such distinctive and individual styles of decoration (**7**). Distribution was also much more localized, though Oxfordshire wares spread right across the Midlands and southern Britain as well as reaching the north in small numbers. Britain was no longer the subject of well-recorded military campaigns, denying us the opportunity to attribute these wares to fairly tight periods. Coinage, though far more numerous, is sometimes less closely datable and more subject to contemporary copying. Cyclical debasement of silver meant that older coin was favoured for savings and thus might be deposited at a time long after the year of striking. These problems affect the understanding of the archaeology of the whole of the third and fourth centuries.

Very few villas are known from the first half century of Roman Britain's existence, for example Fishbourne (Sussex) and Eccles (Kent), though some of the great villas of the fourth century may have had earlier extravagant origins which were absorbed almost undetectably into the late forms. Woodchester (Gloucs), for example, has yielded a small quantity of marble decoration of a type normally associated with the late first and early second century. But this is still the exception rather than the rule. The few early villas were large, and well-appointed, so they almost certainly belonged to romanized tribal chieftains, traders, or Roman officials.

During the second century more and more small villas appeared dotted around the countryside of the south-east, and clearly associated with the burgeoning civitas capitals. Some, such as Rivenhall (Essex) or Park Street (Herts), were built on wealthy pre-Roman sites indicating that the tribal aristocracy had been allowed to retain property which qualified them to participate in cantonal government (though of course the land could have been requisitioned by the state for new owners). Certain areas of the province will have been set aside as imperial estates, exploited for the emperor's personal benefit. Britain, as an imperial province, was a sub-component of the part of the Empire which was the property of the emperor. It was therefore governed by his personal delegate, the *legatus*. Areas such as Salisbury Plain (Wilts) and Cranborne Chase (Dorset) are often cited as places where villas are conspicuous by their absence and it is usually suggested that they were imperial estates. However, there is minimal evidence to prove the point.

Smaller villas began to proliferate in the late third century, reducing the average size. This is important evidence for significantly altered circumstances which might be compared to the emergence of the middle-classes in England during the nineteenth century. This is manifested now in the large quantities of moderately-substantial Victorian houses and the ownership of goods which were the preserve of the rich a century before, such as solid-silver utensils and their imitation in silver-plated form. In both periods the practices of the rich were being emulated by a growing proportion of the population not only because they aspired to do so, but because they now had the resources to acquire the credentials of status. At the same time the rich of Roman Britain began to become wealthy on a comparatively epic scale and it seems that the aristocracy were joining ranks with the cosmopolitan world of the classical elite.

Apart from Britain's developing rural industries, like the Oxfordshire potteries, there were few conspicuous further signs of official development. The existence of several third-century milestones or roadside honorific pillars, such as that of Trajan Decius found at the villa at Rockbourne, show that cantonal governments were capable of administering routine maintenance and sustaining allegiance to the incumbent regime however crudely the scrawled inscriptions on these stones were executed. In some cases these stones are practically the only evidence from Britain (as opposed to the work of ancient geographers like Ptolemy) for the existence of the cantons in the first place. A milestone from Kenchester carries the titles of Numerian for 283–4 and the abbreviation R C D, expandible theoretically as R(espublica) C(ivitatis) D(obunnorum). On Hadrian's Wall the Durotriges are mentioned as contributing to wall building, probably (but far from certainly) in the fourth century. Epigraphically absent from their homeland their building stone from near milecastle 42 at Cawfields seems to record that they had come on the orders of their town at Ilchester. In the towns themselves in contrast urban development seems to have entered a nadir. But, the Romano-British can hardly have failed to be aware of events on the continent, and that they were able to enjoy a complacent sense of detachment despite the effects of contemporary disorder on coinage.

The main Roman silver coin, the *denarius*, relied for its credibility on weight and purity. These fluctuated, but the trend was downwards: both were reduced over successive issues to make the silver go further. Regardless of nominal value older silver probably circulated at a premium. Meanwhile, it took more of the newer, baser, silver to make up enough

8   Silver antoninianus *(double-denarius) of Gordian III (238–44). From the Dorchester South Street hoard of 1933, buried c. 265–85. The reverse is a stock personification of an appropriate virtue, in this case* Laetitia *'Joy'. Diameter 25mm.*

value to pay for the same goods. By 211 the average *denarius* was only around fifty percent silver but it was still sufficiently valuable to play little part in ordinary transactions. This role was served by the large base-metal coins such as the brass *sestertius*, equivalent to one quarter of a denarius, and the *as*, equivalent to one-sixteenth.

Caracalla introduced a new, larger, silver coin distinguished by the use of a radiate crown on the emperor's bust. Today this coin is called the *antoninianus* after Caracalla's official name, or 'radiate'. It was probably valued officially at two *denarii*, but had the silver of just one and a half *denarii* (**8**). This can only have been to make imperial silver stocks go further. To match eighteen denarii for weight, twelve new radiates would be required even if officially only nine would be needed. The superiority of denarii meant that they were preferred for payments of tax, as well as private storage and savings and therefore disappeared from circulation even faster. To begin with the new denomination was produced only sporadically, and was not struck by Severus Alexander (222–35) and Maximinus I (235–8).

Antoniniani were impressive-looking coins in their early days but their deletion from coin types for sixteen years suggests they were associated with declining standards and diminished credibility. Any such fears were well-founded. By the reign of Gordian III the radiate was back and now dominated silver issues at the expense of the denarius. The radiate was progressively debased. By 250 the coins were still visibly silver but the purity had dropped to around a third. At the same time the denarius disappeared altogether. In Britain the effects of a deteriorating coinage may have been worsened by a shortfall in supply. Site finds in Britain of coins from the first half of the third century are relatively rare, including the small change (brass and bronze) of the period, perhaps thanks to erratic supply. Instead there is clear evidence from finds, especially hoards, that the Romano-British were making do with extremely worn coins which were as much as 200 years old.

The Gallic Empire

In 253 Valerian became emperor. He took charge of the East and placed his son Gallienus in charge of the West. To ease his burden and consolidate the dynasty Gallienus placed his own son, Saloninus, in charge of Gaul in 259. The Gauls were insulted by the idea that a boy should rule them so Saloninus was murdered. Postumus, a general in command of the legions on the Rhine, was proclaimed emperor by his troops. Postumus established the Gallic Empire, consisting of Gaul, Spain, and Britain. There was little Gallienus could do because in 260, only a year later, Valerian was captured and imprisoned by the Persians. Gallienus was obliged to deal with the would-be emperors who emerged in the East.

Postumus posed as a legitimate Roman emperor. Two milestones naming him have been found in Britain, one at Trecastle Hill in South Wales, and the other at Brougham in Cumbria. The latter was probably erected by the *civitas* of the Carvetii, probably governed from Carlisle, and shows that north-western Britain was at least prepared to acknowledge his position. The fort at Lancaster was repaired during Postumus' reign, recorded on an inscription which names a governor called Octavius Sabinus and is dated to 262–6. It also bears the names of Gallic Empire consuls and shows that Postumus was maintaining traditional posts and offices, reflected in his coin types. He was murdered in 268 but Britain remained independent of the Empire until 273 under the successive Gallic emperors Marius, Victorinus (**9a**), Tetricus I (**9b**), and his son Tetricus II. Milestones of several of these emperors have been found in Britain, apparently confirming that she was still part of the Gallic Empire. This may be something of an illusion though. The milestones of Victorinus are fairly widely distributed in the north, Wales, and even Huntingdonshire but the stones of the Tetrici are known only in Hampshire. It is quite possible that allegiance to the Gallic Empire was piecemeal and unpredictable. Bitterne, which has produced three of the milestones of Tetricus I (270–3) has also produced one of the two milestones of Aurelian (270–5), the legitimate emperor.

Between roughly the years 259 and 286 the Romano-British were obliged to use predominantly the miserably degenerate coinage of the Gallic Empire. As the intrinsic value of each coin issue declined, so more and more of these silver-washed bronze radiate coins were required to pay for anything. The ridiculous situation eventually developed in which a debased 'silver' radiate had less intrinsic value than a 150-year-old brass *sestertius*, nominally worth only one-eighth of a radiate. Postumus even complicated the situation by issuing his own double-sestertius, often over-struck on first- and second-century examples (**plate 25**). Declining intrinsic value must have been compensated for by an increase in prices requiring correspondingly more coins. Enormous quantities of unofficial copies (now called 'barbarous radiates' or 'radiate copies') were produced, presumably to make it possible to continue transactions in coin, though some were so small and badly made that it seems remarkable they were accepted in exchange for anything. Some had been manufactured by melting down first- second-century brass and bronze coins, an obvious way of making money. Thanks to the discovery of a coin die belonging to an issue from the reign of Tetricus I we know that Silchester's basilica was probably one of the places where they were made, suggesting the activity was at least semi-official.

9   *Left. Bronze radiate of Victorinus (268–70) (obverse only). From the Normanby (Lincs) hoard, found in December 1985. Diameter 18mm.*
      Right. Bronze radiate of Tetricus I (270–3) (obverse only) of the Gallic Empire. Diameter 19mm.

Despite his failure to make any difference to the coinage Postumus had established a very important precedent. He had introduced a workable version of internal secession and shown that the compliance which Rome had relied on to hold her Empire together was no longer something which could be taken for granted, or, if necessary, enforced. Holding back German tribes gave Postumus popularity because he had justified his power to the provincials in his territories. This gave him the backing to fight off Gallienus, and provided his regime with a momentum which allowed it to survive under his successors for another five years. He also utilized stock Roman themes and offices, attempting to validate himself by presenting the regime as a revival of old ways. Being Roman no longer required, it seemed, being ruled from Rome. This was an important psychological change and altered a fact of life into a state of mind. What we must assume is that he enjoyed support amongst the *honestiores*, the wealthy upper-classes, in Britain and Gaul. Had he not done so, his reign could not have been sustained.

The Gallic Empire collapsed during the reign of Aurelian (270–5) whose energetic restoration of the Roman Empire involved suppressing the Palmyran queen Zenobia in the East, as well as Tetricus I in the West. The Gallic Empire was treated magnanimously and with an uncharacteristic lack of violence. Britain's future might have been guaranteed under this reforming regime but Aurelian was murdered in 275 and a succession of brief reigns led to the accession of Probus in 276. Despite his determination to follow Aurelian's reforms Probus was himself murdered in 282. Britain was now faced again with persistent and suicidal instability in Rome, but this time with the knowledge that it was possible to secede from the Roman Empire and yet remain within the military, economic, and social system. There was also a sustained major seaborne threat to her southern and eastern shores which the legitimate regime was unable to deal with. The consequences would turn out to be earth-shattering for Britain and led to her first experiment with independent imperialism of her own.

2 The Carausian Revolt

The Channel protected Britain from the barbarian incursions and imperial civil wars on the continent. But it also served as a highway for pirate attacks on Britain's southern and eastern coasts. To confront the menace new forts were added around the south and east during the third century. Together with the older forts at Brancaster and Reculver they formed a chain of coastal defences mirrored on the north coast of Gaul. The forts, with (usually) right-angled corners, external bastions, and (normally) freestanding walls, resemble those in Gaul. Other contemporary fortifications are known, for example at Cardiff, Holyhead, and Lancaster, built to defend against Irish raiders.

If necessary, older defences and other buildings were removed. At Dover the new fort overlay the second-century fort of the British fleet, the *classis Britannica*. At Richborough (Kent) a monumental arch, which probably commemorated the conquest of Britain, was fortified with ditches to make it into a look-out tower in the mid-third century. Within thirty years the site was cleared, the ditches filled and the colossal walls of the Saxon Shore fort erected.

Eventually the Saxon Shore system in Britain involved at least ten forts (**10**): Brancaster and Burgh Castle (Norfolk), Bradwell (Essex), Reculver, Richborough (**91**), Dover, and Lympne (Kent), Pevensey (Sussex) (**11**), and Portchester (Hants) (**12, plate 2**). A possible eleventh once stood at Walton Castle (Suffolk). If Brancaster and Reculver were earlier, then Burgh Castle was 'transitional' and the others later. The new forts belong to the late third century, and were probably begun under Aurelian or Probus (**13**). Aurelian had embarked on a restoration of military systems and his reign saw the construction of colossal new walls around Rome itself. Burgh Castle has external bastions which are only bonded with the walls from about half-way up. This makes it likely that Burgh Castle was begun without any plan to erect external bastions. As work proceeded bastions were ordered, and work on the ramparts suspended. Once the bastions had reached the height of the walls work continued, and from there on the bastions were bonded in. The fort also had rounded corners and at least two internal towers, characteristics of earlier forts.

The imposing remains at Portchester show the new style of military architecture to good effect but whether the prominent gates and external bastions reflected local tactical requirements or were simply built according to new standard formats is another matter. Excavation revealed that the fort was begun *after* 261 (on the evidence of coins in foundation trenches) but levelling the ground within the walls was still going on more than 25 years later. Pevensey, with its irregular ovoid plan, is generally considered to have been built last, plugging a gap between Lympne and Portchester. Doubts about the very

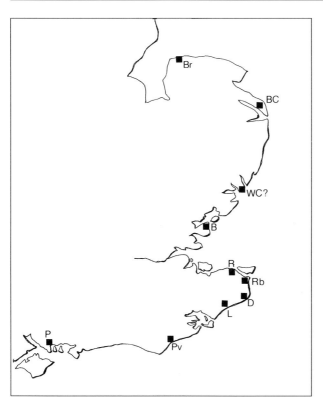

10 Map of south-east Britain
    showing the location of the
    forts of the Saxon Shore.
    Br = Brancaster;
    BC = Burgh Castle;
    WC = Walton Castle;
    B = Bradwell;
    R = Reculver;
    Rb = Richborough;
    D = Dover;
    L = Lympne;
    Pv = Pevensey;
    P = Portchester.

11 *West gate of the Saxon Shore fort at Pevensey (Anderida). The projecting gate-towers are especially characteristic of late Roman military architecture.*

*12   West wall of the Saxon Shore fort at Portchester (*Portus Adurni*).*

limited dating evidence from the site make an accurate date impossible but the presence of Carausian coins at least indicates it was under construction by the late 280s.

Similar forts in Gaul at, for example, Nantes, show that the system was an imperial strategy, and not the result of a usurper's local defensive precautions. They probably served as bases for men, ships, and materials maintained in a state of readiness for dispersal as and when required. Pevensey, for example, stands at the end of a peninsula which once overlooked the sea and, inland, an extensive marsh. Its commanding position remains obvious today and it is clear that it was primarily a maritime base, being difficult to approach and supply by land. The only evidence for the fort garrisons comes from the *Notitia Dignitatum*, a late-fourth-century document itemizing military strengths and garrisons. The forts are listed under a single command, the Count of the Saxon Shore, though when this actually came into existence is unknown. It may have been much later than the forts. Cavalry units are specified at Brancaster and Burgh Castle, and a single legion at Richborough, the II *Augusta*, which had evidently been transferred from Caerleon. The rest were various regular and irregular auxiliary infantry units. Walton Castle seems to have been omitted from the list, perhaps because it was no longer in use. Its loss to coastal erosion means that antiquarian drawings are the only, albeit uncertain, evidence for its existence and role.

The need to defend south-eastern Britain is equally evident in the building of a riverside wall at London in the late third century, reinforced by a look-out tower 0.75 mile (1.2km) downriver at Shadwell. London already had landward walls, as did most of the major Romano-British towns, but these were built much earlier in the third century and

13   *Reformed radiate of Probus (276–82). Probus poses as a consul in a conventional statement of*
    traditional legitimacy. The posture was emulated by usurpers, including Britain's Carausius
    (see **16**). *The reverse depicts* Salus, *the 'health' of the Emperor, plus the Aurelianic XXI*
    statement of value. Struck at Ticinum (Pavia, Italy). Diameter 24mm.

were as much a cosmetic, as a strategic, addition to urban facilities. Building a wall along
the north bank of the Thames was bound to have restricted commerce and must mean
that defence had become an overwhelming priority.

The new forts could have fulfilled other roles, perhaps as prisons (Britain is known to
have been used as a dump for prisoners-of-war in the reign of Probus, see below), and
with control of vagrant bands plaguing Gaul and possibly Britain. The forts may also have
helped protect commerce and imperial supplies by providing secure compounds for food
in transit to the continent. Although pottery and other evidence show that commerce
across the sea carried on into the fourth century they also show that totals diminished and
some goods once imported from the rest of the Empire were now made in Britain. It is,
for instance, interesting that exploitation of the Wealden iron deposits by the *classis
Britannica* had more or less ceased by the period 250–75, something which is certainly not
attributable to the ore being worked out. If it had become harder to ship food and other
resources from Britain the net value of what *was* exported may have increased as demand
outstripped supply. The growth in size of some villas from the late third century shows
that Channel piracy had not prevented the accumulation of wealth; indeed the reverse
may have happened.

Under Probus (**13**), Britain was once again involved in usurpations. In 280 the revolt of
Bonosus, said to be Spanish by birth but British in descent, lasted only one year. Unlikely
to have been more than 30–40 years old, much of his impressionable early adulthood will
have been during the Gallic Empire. His revolt began at Cologne but was crushed by
Probus, who is said to have treated Bonosus' family kindly. The gesture was wasted because
Probus was later confronted by a rebellious governor of Britain whose name is unknown.
This governor had been recommended by a Moor called Victorinus who was sent to
Britain to sort out the problem, as it had been his fault. He used a 'trick', sadly unrecorded,
to remove the troublemaker. Despite these setbacks Probus utilized Britain as a safe-deposit
for prisoners-of-war, taken during battles against 'Vandals' and 'Burgundians'. The

survivors were despatched to Britain where they settled, later serving as Roman troops.

In 282, on the death of Probus, the praetorian prefect Carus became emperor. He made his sons, Numerian and Carinus, associate junior emperors. Carinus was granted the West while his father and brother set off on an eastern campaign. Carus was killed by lightning in 283, an unusually dramatic death even for a Roman emperor, but Numerian was murdered in the customary fashion in 284. Carinus lasted another year and it seems that some time during his brief reign he was obliged to visit Britain. He adopted the title 'Britannicus Maximus', a title which only makes sense if he had won a victory involving Britain. It may have been on the northern frontier, or it may have been in the Channel. Inscriptions bearing his name, and Numerian's, on what were probably milestones, found at respectively Clanville (Hants) and Kenchester (Herefordshire), suggest the regime had effective power in Britain. The commander of the imperial bodyguard, Diocletian, executed Numerian's murderer in 284. That gesture of law and order, uncharacteristic of the age, was followed by Diocletian's own proclamation as emperor in the east which led to supreme power for him when Carinus was murdered.

Carausius

In 284 a soldier called Mausaeus Carausius participated in a war in Gaul against a body of vagrant rebels, called the Bagaudae (or Bacaudae), earning himself a considerable reputation. The forces were led by Maximian, appointed by Diocletian. Carausius had been born around the middle of the third century in Menapia, roughly equivalent to modern Belgium, and spent much of his time at sea though we have no idea whether that was in a civilian or military capacity. Like Bonosus, he spent his formative years in a region controlled by the Gallic Empire, an experience which may have had a significant effect on his ambitions.

The Bagaudae were a disparate sub-class, thrown together by experiences of landlessness, disorder, and barbarian attacks. They finally managed to operate on a cohesive and significant scale in 284, presenting a threat to civil order in Gaul and Diocletian's nascent authority. The revolt was put down by 286 but that required time, manpower, and money which were increasingly regarded as intolerable by the population bearing the impact in the forms of heavy taxation and conscription. In the same year Diocletian made Maximian joint Augustus, giving him control of the West while he took charge of the East.

The problems in the Channel remained unabated. It would take an exceptional man to deal with the threat from 'Franks and Saxons'. Carausius was appointed by Maximian to lead a naval force in the Channel from Boulogne. Despite his background, there was nothing unusual about his rise to fame. In the egalitarian world of Roman military brutality, qualifications of birth had long been replaced by opportunism and ability. The growing plebeian officer class eroded the traditional conflation of Roman military and aristocratic landowning interests but Carausius appears to have cultivated an unusually productive relationship with the Romano-British.

Carausius either planned his rebellion long in advance, or acted on impulse. Maximian came to believe that Carausius was allowing pirates to sail down the Channel to raid in Britain and Gaul first. Then he was believed to be intercepting them on the way home, pocketing a percentage of the 'takings' rather than returning the loot to the rightful owners. This, at any rate, was the story circulated by Maximian but it is equally possible that he had discovered Carausius was becoming popular in Gaul and Britain. Either way Carausius was declared an outlaw and a price put on his head.

Carausius moved decisively so he must have known he had popular support. He declared himself Emperor in Britain and part of Gaul, immediately embarking on a sophisticated public-relations campaign. He avoided challenging the Empire in battle. Instead he presented his domain as the place in which all those neglected Roman civil, military, and religious values would be restored and cherished. Britain was to be not a new Rome but, literally, a refounded old Rome expressed in the language of the great Roman pagan tradition.

Carausian ideology may have been cynical or genuine, but he was a propaganda genius. The civil and military situation in the late third century required little embellishment to be presented as the result of collapsing central authority, and in urgent need of a remedy. Whether or not the Bagaudae were responsible for encouraging wealthy Gallic landowners to take themselves off to Britain is an idea which can neither be proved or disproved, but it would have only enhanced the impression that Diocletian was unable to quash rebellions without considerable difficulty. This would have seemed all the more convincing if pirate raids were carrying on in the Channel.

Carausius, as a self-declared saviour, would have been more easily perceived by the Romano-British as a natural leader than Maximian or Diocletian. With the experience of the Gallic Empire dominating the recollections of everyone over the age of fifteen there would have been little living-memory tradition of rule by a powerful and long-lived emperor based in Rome. It is also likely that a significant number of the *honestiores* found political separation an attractive idea because of the prospects for economic self-preservation.

Carausius knew coinage could make or break his regime. By the time he seized power in 286 the Roman state had virtually ceased to issue bullion coinage in any significant quantity. Older, better, coin had been hoarded away or melted down. Apart from gold, which played little or no part in everyday transactions, other Roman coinage since around 250 had become a motley collection of issues originating under a plethora of different regimes. The only thing they had in common was an almost total absence of silver content, something which damaged imperial credibility as much as it provoked inflation.

Aurelian had tried to restore currency stability. Instead of allowing a coin to fix its value based on the silver content, now coins would bear statements of value making them legal tender at that nominal value. Aurelian's reformed 'silver' coins bore the cryptic mark XXI, probably indicating the proportion of bronze to silver (20:1), or that the new coin was valued at twenty old *sestertii*. Some of the silver content was used to create a surface silver 'wash' which will have made these new coins look quite respectable. Few found their way across the Channel. Britain relied instead on Gallic Empire coinage, and the vast quantities of degenerate second- and third-generation radiate copies. These circulated (and were discarded) to such an extent that they dominate site finds to this day.

Carausius started producing bronze radiate coinage as soon as his reign began. This guaranteed that his image and name was circulated widely and fast, though these issues

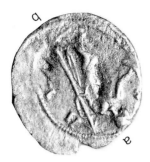 

14   Left. Obverse of a radiate coin of Gallienus (253–68) over-struck with a Carausian radiate
     reverse. a–b marks the axis of the Carausian figure of PAX. The other side depicts Carausius'
     portrait over-struck on the Gallienus reverse. Diameter 22mm.
     Right. Obverse of a radiate coin of Tetricus I (270–3) over-struck with a Carausian radiate
     (reverse). a–b marks the axis of the Carausian figure of PAX. The other side depicts
     Carausius' portrait over-struck on the Tetricus reverse. Diameter 21mm.

lacked the five percent silver of Aurelian's reformed radiates. The work began before there
had been time to manufacture coin blanks for striking. Instead, his mint-workers used
coinage then in circulation, including radiates of Gallienus and barbarous radiates of the
Gallic Empire. On them Carausius' image can be seen, crudely over-struck on the reused
coins (**14**).

But, knowing full well that his credibility amongst the British garrison was at stake,
Carausius ordered new gold and silver coins, perhaps using the booty he had been accused
of appropriating. At 90 percent purity the silver coins were prepared to a standard
unknown since the reign of Nero, 220 years before. Compared to the best the legitimate
Empire could produce Carausian silver was spectacular but in Britain, where the
miserable coins of the Gallic Empire dominated the circulating coinage, they must have
been even more impressive. The psychological impact of producing high-quality silver
and gold cannot be underestimated. In the Roman world it was, literally, synonymous
with legitimacy.

The new silver was probably issued at ceremonies to soldiers or officials who had
committed themselves to Carausius. The reverses depicted a variety of solid Roman
virtues: Carausius was 'restorer of the Romans', the faithfulness of the army was
proclaimed, and so on. In one remarkable issue he presented himself in a messianic
posture, unprecedented for a Roman emperor, by adapting a line from Virgil's *Aeneid*. On
these coins, Carausius was 'the awaited one', welcomed by Britannia (*Expectate veni*,
'Come, awaited one'). This intriguing brag suggests that when Carausius seized power
there was already an undercurrent of discontent.

But the most sophisticated element was confined to the bottom part of the reverses, the
'exergue'. Here the letters RSR were placed on most of the silver, some of the gold, and a
very few bronze radiates. This is where normally an abbreviated form of the mint city was

15   Top. *Bronze radiate of Carausius (286–93) bearing, unusually, RSR (in this case retrograde,
      or running backwards) on the reverse. The reverse depicts Carausius on horseback and the
      legend* Adventus Aug[usti], *'the coming of the Emperor'. Diameter 19mm.*
      Bottom. *Bronze radiate of Carausius. On the reverse is a galley and the legend* Felicitas
      Aug[usti], *a type first struck under Hadrian and also used by Postumus. The mintmark
      reads CXXI, denoting the unlocated 'C' mint and the Aurelianic statement of value (see text).
      Diameter 24mm.*

located, for example ML for *Moneta Londinii* (a mint founded by Carausius), or one of the
Aurelianic statements of value (**15, 18**). So, it was assumed until recently that RSR stood
either for a mint, which was unidentifiable, or perhaps a financial official, the *Rationalis
Summae Rei*. The latter made better sense because Carausius had an official called Allectus
described as holding a similar, but not identical, title.

The letters RSR happen also to correspond with the initial letters of *Redeunt Saturnia
Regna*, a line from Virgil's profound, and messianic, poem known as the Fourth Eclogue.
It means literally 'The Saturnian Reigns return' (equivalent to 'The Golden Age is back')
based on a colloquial expression, derived from the myth that the earliest days of the world
had been a peaceful bucolic paradise ruled by Saturn. This convenient association of the
letters might very well be regarded as coincidence. But two unique medallions, in bronze,
of Carausius have survived (**16**). One bears RSR on the bottom of the reverse. The other
bears the letters INPCDA in the same place. The latter have defied interpretation until
recently. But, the line following *Redeunt Saturnia Regna* in Virgil's Fourth Eclogue reads
Iam Nova Progenies Caelo Demittitur Alto. This means, 'Now a new generation is let down

16   *Top. Bronze medallion of Carausius in consular garb with an eagle-tipped sceptre in his right hand. On the reverse he stands facing left in military dress with Victory with the legend VICTOR CARAVSIVS AVG GERM MAX, with the initials RSR for Redeunt Saturnia Regna (Virgil,* Eclogues *iv.6; see text). Diameter 35mm. (Copyright — The British Museum.)*

    Bottom. Bronze medallion of Carausius in consular garb as **15**. *On the reverse Victory in a chariot galloping with the legend VICTORIA CARAVSI AVG, and the initials I.N.P.C.D.A. for Iam Nova Progenies Caelo Demittitur Alto (Virgil,* Eclogues *iv.7; see text). Diameter 36mm. (Copyright — The British Museum.)*

from Heaven above'. Not only do the letters correspond but the meaning is precisely appropriate to Carausius' more explicit and conventional messages on the coins. The chances against this being coincidence are astronomical. Moreover, reducing stock phrases and formulae to initial form was customary in the Roman world. The phrases were almost certainly used in Carausian panegyrics which, of course, do not survive. Similar literary allusions can be found in the extant panegyrics for legitimate emperors of the period.

There is no other such verbal reference to Virgil's works on any other Latin Roman coin (as opposed to those struck in the Greek-speaking cities of the eastern part of the Empire). Virgil wrote the *Eclogues* in the latter part of the first century BC, more than 300 years before. He supported Augustus and had been an integral part of developing the legendary origins of the Empire founded in an unequivocal association of empire with traditional pagan Roman religion and myth. His works had since become standard Latin school fare and were drilled into every child who attended school in the Roman Empire.

Carausius was utilizing a popular theme which had conveniently wide and subliminal associations in literature and general contemporary religious belief. It was a means by which he could link himself with more elevated feelings than shameless military opportunism. Carausius, or at any rate his supporters, realized that by subtly appealing to this knowledge he could associate himself with ancient Roman tradition. Identifying emperors with mythical figures was routine in the Roman world but in the third and fourth centuries this became more pronounced. Diocletian and Maximian were presented as Jupiter and Hercules on coins, and associated with them in the panegyrics, for example; but, no other usurper of this, or any other period in antiquity, showed himself to be so in command of an ideological base as Carausius.

That Carausius felt able to exploit this seam of traditional belief in Britain, an outpost of the Empire, tells us much about what Britain had become. When Virgil wrote, his works would have been incomprehensible to the illiterate, Celtic-speaking, Britons. If knowledge of Virgil could be exploited in the late third century then Roman Britain now had an educated, latinized, elite who measured themselves by their appreciation of traditional Roman values. This has implications for our understanding of Britain in the fourth century and in many ways this is the first real signpost to the nature of the maturing province. However, there is an important distinction to be made here. Stating that the Romano-British elite were familiar with classical literature and imagery is not the same as saying that they indulged their lives in esoteric philosophical detachment from the world around them. But it does mean saying that the slogans, metaphors, allegories and images they utilized to decorate their environment, speech and thoughts were drawn from the classical canon.

When his reign began Carausius was striking coins at Rouen, indicating that he controlled northern Gaul as well as Britain, though the Rouen issues may have come before taking power in Britain. Even the biased official accounts fail to mention any hostility to him in Britain itself. An impression must have circulated amongst some of the garrison of Roman Britain in their run-down forts that the Empire was unconcerned with them. Low morale and the prospect of excitement probably stimulated their support, while the troops who had been sent to Britain as prisoners-of-war under Probus are unlikely to have taken much persuading. Good silver would have guaranteed allegiance. One clue comes from the fact that although he issued bronze coins in the names of some of the legions in Britain and northern Europe, he omitted the VI *Victrix*, the legion based at York and under the command of the governor who controlled *Britannia Inferior*. Perhaps the governor and legion had not transferred their allegiance to Carausius. But the only inscription which mentions Carausius is a milestone from near Carlisle, an important town within the northern region, presumably therefore under Carausius' control (**17**). It is extremely unlikely that the milestone was unusual at the time, and its survival reflects the remoteness of the region.

Most Carausian bronze radiate coins have reverses depicting Pax with the simple legend PAX AVG. Many have no mint-mark and those which do came from the London mint, or the 'C' mint which may be either *Camulodunum* (Colchester) or *Corinium* (Cirencester), though there are other possibilities (**15**). It is remarkable that his name is almost never blundered, even on coins where the reverse legend is garbled. The coins suggest that

17 *Milestone from Gallows Hill, 1 mile*
    (1.6km) south of Carlisle. The upper end
    bears the dedication to Carausius, the
    'unconquered Augustus' (probably 290–93).
    The stone is the only source of expansion for
    Carausius' initial 'M' as Maus[aeus?]. The
    other end carries the dedication to Constantine
    as Caesar (306–7). Height 1.88m. Now at
    Tullie House Museum, Carlisle.
    Height 1.87m. (RIB 2290–2).

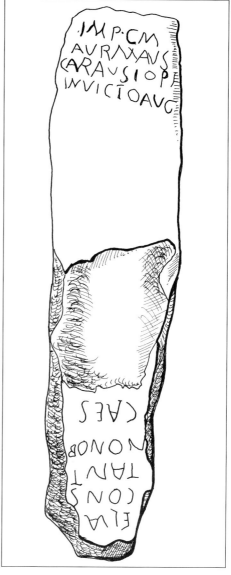

London was Carausius' administrative base. Die-links (coins struck from the same dies) show that some coins bearing the RSR mark on the reverse, had obverses struck from dies also used on coins with the London mint-mark on the reverse. The 'C' mint coins are different in style, suggesting a different location. Colchester would have been attractive to Carausius, particularly given its origins as the first major town of Roman Britain. But it is impossible to extrapolate beyond this to associate him with the physical remains of Roman Britain. Many of the Saxon Shore forts, like Portchester, have produced enough coins of the reign to suggest that building activity there continued unabated. We cannot say in any instance that he was responsible for initiating construction, though it would clearly have been in his interests to maintain building work.

Support for Carausius must have come from those who had most to lose by remaining in the legitimate Empire. From around the 270s onwards villas began to increase and a small number were enlarged and embellished in a spurt of growth which extended well on into the fourth century. There was a pattern of revolts in the fourth century which invariably involved Romano-British support of some sort and the literary records occasionally imply that the *honestiores* of Britain had participated. Perhaps a trend had emerged in which some of the Romano-British elite saw their best chances in political detachment from the Roman world, but had no desire for cultural or economic severance.

An analogy from a different time and place shows us how significant the economic and social self-interest of a minority can be. In the southern states of the USA in the early 1800s the economic and political interest in maintaining slavery, dressed up as a defence of state liberty and the maintenance of a balance of power in the Union government, led to the secession, state by state, of a region from the greater whole. The dominant members of city and state governments were, in many cases, the minority large-scale landowners who had most to lose from remaining in a union in a progressively anti-slavery climate. They had the support of the majority of the mostly very-poor white population who depended on them. Despite the secession, the Confederate government, far from doing away with the offices and institutions of the very system which had been rejected, proceeded to ape many of them. Their world was also characterized by a reactionary admiration for European, especially English, culture.

The parallels with Roman Britain are interesting. Perhaps rural development, the growing wealth of a few, and the emergence of usurpers were symptoms of the same trend. As Britain grew richer so she became worth attacking and, at the same time, she became a viable independent political domain. Her elite would have found the idea of sacrificing their wealth to pay taxes which funded military campaigns on the continent unacceptable. Carausius emerged as the man best-placed to protect them both from taxes and the privations of barbarians. Their wealth, and relative insulation from military disasters on the continent, may also have created a desire to secede from a system which threatened their status. It is unlikely that Carausius, or his associates, had not recognized in advance that his appealing conjunction of rhetoric and economic interest would be welcomed.

Whether Carausius succeeded in creating an efficient process of government or whether the regime operated on an ad-hoc basis is unknown. That his successor, Allectus, was described as a high official, connected probably with financial affairs, suggests there was a formal administration. Carausian panegyrics, probably alluded to by the Virgilian slogans on the RSR and INPCDA coins, would have been read out to troops, or perhaps in public places. Some of his coins have reverses depicting the emperor on horseback with the legend *Adventus Aug[usti]*, 'the coming of the Emperor'. This was a standard theme, issued to record imperial visits (**15**). Carausian versions, as normal, do not specify the location but it would be very unlikely that they did not record real visits by him to major towns or military bases in Britain to reinforce his rule. The *Adventus* types also appear on some of the silver RSR coins and had perhaps been handed out on such occasions.

The importance of sustaining military support may have led Carausius to neglect civilian government. With only the Carlisle milestone to work from it is impossible to judge. The unique medallions, and some coinage, depict Carausius as a consul. Numismatists believe that Carausius awarded himself consulships in 287 and 289, based on detailed studies of the coin legends. The consulship, the most important magistracy which any Roman could hold, was not to be treated lightly. Carausius was posing as the ultimate legitimate Roman ruler in a context which will have outraged Diocletian and Maximian. He even adopted the forenames Marcus Aurelius, a convention devised by Caracalla in the early third century to claim pseudo-descent from the house of the deified Emperor Marcus Aurelius.

Around 289 an invasion of Britain was prepared, recorded in a panegyric to Maximian. It describes how promising weather conditions were followed by catastrophic storms which destroyed the campaign before it had begun. Carausius remained in power, and a subsequent panegyric of 291 makes no mention of the aborted invasion. Maximian was obliged to negotiate a peace. For the moment Carausius enjoyed naval supremacy in the Channel.

In 293 Diocletian and Maximian appointed assistants and heirs. This system was known as the Tetrarchy. In the west Maximian was joined by Constantius Chlorus, who was ordered to recover Britain. Carausius was aware of the plans. He issued an extraordinary series of bronze coins bearing his bust alongside those of Diocletian and Maximian with the optimistically-conciliatory legend *Carausius et Fratres Sui* ('Carausius and his Brothers'). He also issued coins in their sole names, but with reverse legends ending AVGGG, a convention indicating three Augusti. Carausius had evidently decided to pose as a legitimate member of Diocletian's multi-ruler system, in spite of flaunting himself as a consul. But Carausius had presented Diocletian and Maximian with no choice. Tolerating him would be an admission of weakness which would destroy their prestige and threaten their reforms.

In 293 Constantius blockaded Boulogne harbour and retook the city. The setback might have destroyed Carausius' reputation. If the *Fratres* conciliation coins were part of change in policy, that new strategy might have contributed to a power struggle within Carausius' command. He was murdered by, or on the orders of, Allectus who then became emperor in Britain. Carausius disappears from our picture of history instantly. This raises the possibility that Carausius and Allectus were just the visible faces of a cabal, something implied in a panegyric recording the eventual defeat of the regime, now riven by internal disputes. Allectus issued his own coins but the allusions to classical literature and the conciliation coins were never revived. Silver was not issued (at least, none has ever been found), but Allectus maintained an output of good-quality gold and even introduced a smaller bronze coin, known as a *quinarius*.

This points to dogmatic maintenance of an independent Britain and a rejection of assumed membership of the imperial college. The mint-marks on Allectan coinage continued the sequences begun by Carausius, showing that London and the 'C' mint remained in use (**18**). Allectus kept up a programme of public appearances, recorded on gold coins with the legend *Adventus Aug[usti]*. Some of the bronze coins indicate that he also appointed himself to a consulship, but any hints of a messianic coming or a revival of a mythical pagan paradise were abandoned. Carausian coins are distinguished by a careless but ebullient style, depicting the hero as a flamboyant thug. Allectan coins are, by contrast, conventional and better made. The revolt may have endured for the moment but it had lost its spirit.

18   *Bronze radiate of Allectus (293–6). The reverse depicts* Pax *('Peace') and the mint-mark for London* (M[oneta] L[ondinii]). *Diameter 22mm.*

In London a monumental building was begun using timber now said to have been felled in 294. It has been suggested that this might have been Allectus' headquarters. The idea seems reasonable enough; after all, Allectus struck coins at London and was probably based there. But such an attractive association is untenable and ultimately pointless, given the limitations of the current evidence. The wood may have been allowed to season for several years before it was used, so it may not have been contemporary. Allectus must have had powerful supporters, any of whom (or none) might have been responsible. The best evidence for an association with the regime is the fact that it was abandoned before completion.

Even if Allectus was still able to count on Romano-British support he must have been aware of the impending invasion. Allectan coinage is found in Gaul which proves that there was some traffic, probably commercial, but he may have retained a power base of sorts. The subsequent restoration of Hadrian's Wall forts might suggest that troops had been pulled *en masse* to bolster his defences. However, an inscription of 296–305 at Birdoswald describes a fort ruined by natural decay (see below). The dislocated central authority of the late third century make a more plausible background to long-term decay.

Once Constantius had been able to quash barbarians in the Rhineland he was able to begin the campaign against Britain. The panegyric of 297 describes Britain as a startlingly fertile and mineral-rich province, going on to describe how it had been the Romans who had brought civilisation to this outpost of the known world. Of course Britain was inevitably going to be described as immensely valuable. Even if Britain was in reality a liability, no self-respecting panegyricist was going to say so. As Florus pronounced so many years before, Britain and its romanization was a trophy. It could not be abandoned because of the damage to prestige.

The assault on Allectan Britain was launched in two waves, despite bad weather. Constantius sailed from Boulogne and Asclepiodotus, the praetorian prefect, from the Seine. Hidden by fog, Asclepiodotus and his force were able to pass the Isle of Wight without being spotted by the Allectan navy. He landed, presumably in the Southampton area, burnt his fleet and marched inland. Thanks either to the surprise or disorganization Allectus had failed to gather his forces. He fled inland, abandoning another fleet under his command, with whatever units he was able to amass at a moment's notice. These seem to have been mainly mercenaries. Asclepiodotus caught up with Allectus and they fought a battle in which Allectus was defeated and killed.

Afterwards, Constantius' half of the force eventually reached Britain and seized London. This was presented as a triumphal entry on a well-known gold medallion struck to commemorate the event, and very likely awarded to a participant in the campaign. Constantius is depicted in *adventus* mode, but this time with the legend *redditor lucis aeternae*, 'restorer of the eternal light'. The mounted Constantius and a war galley alongside are welcomed by a figure standing outside a city gate. The letters LON make it clear that London is meant. The defeat had been total. Britain's first experiment at empire was over, but the *honestiores* remained in control of the Romano-British landscape.

3 Restoration of the eternal light

Constantius' panegyricist described the Britons as being overwhelmed with joy at their liberation in 296. He was bound to of course, and it is just as obvious that it cannot have been entirely true. Although the Romano-British may have become sceptical about the Carausian regime, at the beginning they probably welcomed it. But Constantius denied himself an excuse to treat the Britons harshly by posing as a liberator and restorer of the 'eternal light'.

The rebel regime was given the usual bad press: the Britons had been held in captivity, their wives had suffered outrages, and their children had been enslaved. Constantius was naturally by comparison the sheer embodiment of reason, beneficence and enlightenment. The names of Carausius and Allectus were omitted from the panegyric, and they were referred to as pirates and ringleaders. There is no suggestion of a division in Britain between pro- and anti-rebellion which Constantius could exploit. This makes it more likely that the revolt had been broadly popular. The panegyric also proclaimed that the Britons were once more Roman, and another trumpeted that the Saturnian Golden Age had been finally reborn under Diocletian and Maximian. As Carausius had claimed precisely such an achievement, recorded on his coinage, the panegyricists were obviously trying to sink Carausian propaganda. This promise of a return to 'old values' was a relentless theme of the later Empire anticipated by earlier usurpers such as Postumus and one with which we are just as familiar in our own time.

A pogrom in Britain may have been ordered, but Allectus himself might already have cleared out Carausius' most loyal supporters. Alienating the Romano-British elite would have been risky for Constantius. At the Piddington villa (Northants) a programme of restoration ceased about now, leaving plastered walls unpainted and piles of tesserae unused. A coin of Allectus under a new floor shows that the work was underway in the mid-290s or somewhat later. The excavators have speculated that the owners were supporters of Allectus, and were replaced by occupants who lit fires on the floors and left animal remains by the walls. Such conditions are often interpreted as evidence for 'squatter occupation', but the possibility that the 'squatters' were the original, though impoverished, owners is rarely considered. At Fishbourne a restoration of the first-century palace was ended by a major fire and was never resumed (**19**). Of course the Allectan coin at Piddington only dates the laying of the floor, and subsequently the abandonment, to *after* 296 while the Fishbourne fire may have been purely accidental. The reasons for changes in ownership or abandonment of renovations in either case may have been personal ruin as a result of individual circumstances, and a general association of dates cannot be treated as more than coincidental.

*19   Hypocaust at Fishbourne (West Sussex) installed in the north wing at the end of the third
century. It was unused at the time of the house's destruction by fire shortly afterwards.*

However, an interesting perspective on the archaeological evidence at Piddington and
Fishbourne is a comment in an imperial panegyric of about 297. A number of *artifices*
(skilled workers) were taken from Britain *quibus illae provinciae redundabant*, 'with whom
the provinces were overflowing', to work on the restoration of Autun which had been
ravaged by war. In an age of requisitioned labour and other coercive provisions this was
not only easy to arrange but might have had far-reaching consequences for projects
currently in hand in Britain. It also provides us with an interesting glimpse of the skilled
workforce available and thus a background to the development of villa culture.

Diocletian believed that the Empire could now only be held together by coercion and
delegation. Passive acquiescence to imperial authority was a thing of the past. His edict on
maximum prices, issued in 296, is perhaps the most vivid and well-known of his
measures. Sustaining the state at any cost was an all-consuming priority and Britain was
clearly a province with a worrying capacity for independence. The 'uncontrolled madmen'
cursed by Diocletian in the edict no doubt included Carausius who had shown that
Britain had achieved an identity which was more sophisticated than a revival of Celtic
tribal fantasies of liberation. Had there been even the slightest trace of a pre-Roman tribal
flavour to popular Romano-British self-regard, Carausius would have exploited it. That
he did not tells us an enormous amount about what had happened to Britain since the
Roman invasion in 43. The influential members of the Romano-British community now
saw themselves as Romans first. The idea that Britain was a persistently reactionary

province, labouring under a superficial Roman yoke, seems increasingly unlikely. What led to the Carausian revolt may have been connected with what led to the changes we can see in the Romano-British countryside.

The machinations of the Tetrarchic power struggles were largely irrelevant to Britain. Diocletian's plans that he and Maximian abdicate in favour of Galerius and Constantius were doomed though Maximian complied to begin with. In 305 Constantius I became Augustus in the West, and Galerius in the East. Diocletian wanted to separate permanently civilian and military administration. The Empire was split into regional commands controlled by praetorian prefects. These commands were subdivided into dioceses. Each diocese was controlled by a *vicarius*, literally the praetorian prefect's proxy. Britain was a diocese by 319 when its vicar was a man called Pacatianus (recorded in an edict of that year), and fell into the prefecture of the Gauls along with northern Gaul (including Germany), south Gaul, and Spain. The prefecture came to be controlled from Trier.

Britain was certainly subdivided into four provinces by 312, recorded in a document called 'Names of all the Provinces' (*Nomina Provinciarum Omnium*, also known as the Verona List), compiled in 312–14. Like the division of Britain under Severus a century before this must have been devised to increase government control, and to diminish further the chances of any more usurpations. She became *Britannia Prima* (south-west including Wales), *Maxima Caesariensis* (south-east), *Flavia Caesariensis* (north Midlands), and *Britannia Secunda* (north). The first two seem to have been made out of *Britannia Superior* and the latter two out of *Britannia Inferior*. The exact boundaries are unknown. *Maxima* was governed by a man of consular rank, indicating its primacy, while the others were governed by a *praeses*, literally 'the official in charge', a later Latin word for a provincial governor (as opposed to the old *legatus*).

The fifth-century document *Notitia Dignitatum* (Compendium of Great Offices of State) lists the various civil and military commands of the Empire. It provides details of the British garrison as far back as the early 300s but was compiled over a long time. As a result it is very difficult to be sure which references belong to which period, though it is believed generally to refer to affairs after 368.

The armies in Britain and elsewhere were divided between the static frontier garrisons, *limitanei*, and the mobile field army, *comitatenses*, controlled by the Emperor. Britain had two *limitaneus* garrisons. The *Dux* (Duke), based at York, commanded one, subdivided into the units in the forts of north-east Britain, and units in forts on Hadrian's Wall and across north-western Britain. Rather oddly, the other was controlled by the *Comes* (Count) of the Saxon Shore, *comes* being a commanding rank normally associated with the field army. In addition, the Count of the Britons commanded a wing of the field army consisting of six cavalry and three infantry units. A chance reference tells us that the Emperor Valentinian's father, Gratian, held this post. As part of the field army it may not even have been stationed permanently in Britain, reminding us that the *Notitia* is only a collage of snap-shots.

Part of establishing the new system involved reconstructing Britain's northern defences. Between 296–305 the Wall fort at Birdoswald was restored, recorded in an inscription which describes how the commandant's house was so ruinous that it was covered in earth and that it, the headquarters building, and the baths, were rebuilt during the governorship

20 *Inscription of c. 296–305, recording building work at Birdoswald. The names of the
    Tetrarchy: Diocletian, Maximian, Constantius and Galerius, are in the first three lines.
    Galerius is referred to by his* cognomen *(Maximian) as are the others. We use his*
    praenomen *to distinguish him from Maximian. The name of the governor Aur[elius]
    Arpagius is in the fourth line. Diameter 838mm. (RIB 1912.)*

of Aurelius Arpagius (**20**). A fragment of a similar inscription at Housesteads almost
certainly records similar work there at the same date. Arpagius, despite being the governor,
is also described as being in control of the army — the division of responsibility had not
yet occurred in Britain. He probably governed *Britannia Inferior* or, if the further
subdivision had taken place, *Britannia Secunda*. Perhaps, breaking with normal policy, the
governor was given an unusual range of powers across all of Britain to guarantee that
imperial authority was enforced across the whole island.

   Arpagius is the last governor of Britain testified on an inscription. With him the world
of datable Roman military inscriptions in Britain ends for good. No military event or
personality recorded in fourth-century histories can be associated with a specific site.
Trying to reconcile the *Notitia* with archaeology has been a bumpy ride. At Caerleon,
fortress of the II legion *Augusta*, the last piece of datable building work belongs to the
reign of Aurelian. The garrison, or what passed for one, had moved to Richborough in
the fourth century, according to the *Notitia*. Caerleon was abandoned and partly
demolished. York, headquarters of the VI legion *Victrix*, also capital of *Britannia Inferior*
and its successor *Britannia Secunda*, had a different fate. The walls of the legionary fortress

facing the river were embellished with external multangular towers. This was probably because the Duke was based here and needed a prestigious base. However, minimal evidence from within the fortifications points to a reduced garrison and some dereliction. Meanwhile, the XX legion *Valeria Victrix* at Chester disappears from the record for good after Carausius.

The Wall fort of Haltonchesters is described by the *Notitia* as occupied but no evidence of late-fourth-century activity has been found. Other forts, such as Lancaster, which were apparently occupied are omitted from the list. The weakness here is likely to be archaeology. Short-term occupation of part of a fort might very well have left little or no evidence detectable in the ground, especially when few forts have been completely excavated. The II legion's presence at Richborough has to be taken on trust because there is nothing from Richborough to settle the point. All that can be said is that the *Notitia* represents a hotchpotch of information available to hand in the early fifth century, much of which will have been out of date and may be right or wrong.

The late army was supplemented with *foederati* and *laeti*, neither of which come from romanized provinces. *Laeti* were barbarians who had surrendered to the Empire and in return were allowed to settle within its boundaries, so long as they supplied men for the Roman army. The *foederati* had not surrendered but had made a kind of contract to fight for the Empire on a unit basis. Unlike the *laeti*, the *foederati* hung on to their names and unit identities. There is no suggestion that any of these 'barbarian' Roman troops were inferior to their predecessors but likely consequences would be a lack of instinctive loyalty to the legitimate state.

The old sense of purpose of Roman destiny had been replaced by an ill-paid obligation to face increasingly long odds. Many older auxiliary units had been stationed in the same forts for so long that very few of their members could have even been to nominal homelands like Thrace and Batavia. Few had seen action of any consequence. The late-third and fourth centuries created a tradition of military disasters for the British garrison which was drawn on by usurpers or emperors who wanted reinforcements. Detachments of British legions are testified on the continent during the reign of Gallienus and probably never returned. Reduction is reflected in the reduced capacity of barrack buildings in some of the Wall forts. Fourth-century Richborough, accommodating the II legion, had less than one-sixth the internal area of the legion's old base at Caerleon.

Britain was a military backwater, but for some officers life could still be good. At South Shields, following a late-third-century fire, the fort was rebuilt with new barracks and a commanding officer's courtyard house in Mediterranean style. At some other northern forts, such as Housesteads, new barracks replaced the old strips of rooms. But, Housesteads is also one of several Wall forts which was steadily deteriorating. Eventually the ramparts were clumsily repaired with stones and some of the gates were dismantled and blocked up, in one case being converted into a jerry-built wooden affair wedged into what was left of the monumental Hadrianic gate.

Roman military equipment seems to have become more diverse by the late third century (**21**), and much rarer in the fourth century. Late equipment may have been more highly-valued, and thus better looked after; alternatively it may have been harder to come by in Britain. As a result the finds from such military sites resemble the detritus of civilian

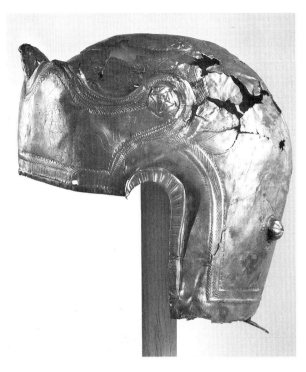

21 *Bronze cavalry 'sports' helmet from Guisborough (Yorks). Designed for show the helmet is decorated with figures of Mars, Minerva, and Victory. Late third century. (Copyright — The British Museum.)*

sites and are thus not automatically recognizable as military areas. Distinctive fourth-century metalwork in some graves, for example at Lankhills, Winchester, and Dorchester-on-Thames (**22**), was once thought to show that Germanic *foederati* had been employed in Britain even though the locations make this most unlikely. However, the *Notitia* does refer to Saxon units in the late Roman army. The reality of the late-Roman frontier army will have been disparate troops with an infinite variety of ethnic origins and equipment, and difficult to categorize on the basis of artefacts.

In the fourth century then there was a fragmented and demoralized garrison in Britain. The total was perhaps only a quarter of the numbers 200 years before. In practice even this will have been permanently compromised by sickness, desertion, indifference and incompetence. A force of this size was not only unlikely to have much effect in dealing with sustained barbarian incursions but an ambitious usurper could have reduced it to almost zero in very short order.

Military loyalty and political credibility, as Carausius knew, depended on a sound coinage. Diocletian issued a silver coin of his own, the *argenteus*, which resembled Carausian silver in size and weight. It was never popular and fell out of use. An oddity of the late Empire is that only Britain and Dacia seem to have favoured silver denominations for savings. Carausian and Allectan coins may have been demonetized in 296, along with all the forms of earlier radiates, but it was not unknown for Roman money-changers to refuse to accept coins issued by usurpers. A papyrus from Egypt, of about 260, records an edict requiring money-changers to accept all coin except forgeries and suspect pieces, but this kind of enactment was probably difficult to enforce. The reason the medallions of Carausius (**16**) are individually unique is probably because they are chance survivals of

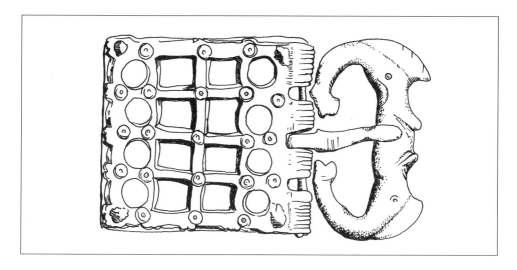

22   *Late bronze belt buckle. The idea that these buckles prove of the presence of Germanic mercenaries has been discounted. Nevertheless they are commonest in frontier provinces and may have had a general military or official association. From Dorchester-on-Thames (Oxon). Late fourth century. Length 90mm. (After Vinciguerra.)*

coins which were generally disposed of once it became expedient to sever any visible links with the regime, especially if they had been donatives for loyal supporters.

The mint of London was maintained, but to begin with, the mint-mark ML (*Moneta Londinii*) was omitted from the new Tetrarchy coins (**23**). When restored it was in a new version, PLN (*Pecunia LoNdinii*) (**plate 25**), thus avoiding a direct legacy of the rebellion. The new coins belong to mainstream issues which appeared all over the Empire. Now known as a *follis* the dominant type bears the legend *Genio Populi Romani*, 'To the Genius of the Roman People' (**plate 25**). It was issued across the Roman world in identical form apart from mint-marks. Much larger than a radiate, even Carausius' most extravagant versions, and of a far more regular weight, the new coin had the visual advantage of a silver wash (almost always absent from surviving examples). These coins are rare in Britain, probably because their value made them worth recovering if lost, though if used for military wages it is possible that payments made to the Romano-British garrison were erratic. Even if these coins restored financial stability it was short-lived. As the Tetrarchic system crumbled so did the reliability of the coinage. Within a few years issues of reduced standard, and more variation in type, began to appear.

Constantius in northern Britain

In 305 Constantius came to Britain to campaign in the north, either to punish barbarians or to conquer new territory. The Birdoswald inscription, if taken literally, suggests there had been little trouble in the north in recent years. A panegyric records the trip, complimenting the emperor for not attempting to occupy Scotland, Ireland or 'Thule' (a term for the semi-mythical lands to the far north), and instead indulging himself with the

23   *Bronze coin of Maximian, probably struck at London between 296–305. The reverse depicts
a stock theme:* Genio Populi Romani, *'To the Genius of the Roman People'.
Diameter 26mm.*

metaphysical experience of witnessing the midsummer midnight sun as a foretaste of the
afterlife. Poetically appealing that may be, it supplies no information about the campaign
apart from implying it might have been unsuccessful. But Constantius died shortly
afterwards and could have been suffering from a terminal illness causing at least a certain
amount of reflective soul-searching.

Constantius had had two wives. Helena, his first, produced a son, Constantine, who
was born at Naissus in Dalmatia about the year 285. Within four years Constantius
effectively divorced her (there is no evidence they were legitimately married) and married
Theodora, the step-daughter of Maximian. Constantine remained associated with his
father, presenting a dynastic threat to Galerius. Galerius decided to promote his own
family and had already appointed both the new Caesars, one of whom was his nephew.
Constantine felt his birthright was being stolen and set out to Britain to meet Constantius,
being detained on the way by Galerius. He escaped and reached Britain in 306.

On 25 July 306 Constantius died at York. The army there declared Constantine
emperor, an act which had unimaginable consequences for the history of the western
world, but much of what followed took place beyond Britain. Diocletian's radical system
of governing the Empire was beginning to serve as a portent for the inter-dynastic
wrangling of medieval Europe. Nonetheless a fragmentary inscription from the
mithraeum in London recording four emperors evidently belongs to this period and is
usually attributed to the years 307–8. Apart from the milestones it is the last inscription to
refer to imperial authority in Roman Britain. In 312, at the Battle of the Milvian Bridge in
Italy, Constantine defeated and killed Maxentius. The Empire was secured for
Constantine and his associate Licinius, a former member of Galerius' army. Constantine
professed that he had no doubt the victory was thanks to the Christian god and in 313 he
and Licinius issued the Edict of Milan which guaranteed total religious toleration. In 324
Constantine fought against Licinius and defeated him, thereby seizing supreme power.

24   *Milestone from St Hilary (Cornwall)*
     church with the titles of Constantine I
     as Caesar, son of the deified
     Constantius, for the years 306–7.
     Height 1.27m above the church floor.
     (RIB 2233).

Meanwhile in Britain the Carlisle milestone of Carausius had been unceremoniously inverted and carved with the name of Constantine I, as Caesar, a title he held between 306–7. The milestone must have remained exposed with the name of Carausius for around a decade after the defeat of Allectus (**17**). Although Carausius' name was buried it is interesting that no effort was made to erase his name, the normal practice for someone consigned to *damnatio memoriae* ('the damnation of [his] memory'). It remains the sole epigraphic record of his rule.

Most surviving inscriptions from Roman Britain from the early fourth century appear on inscribed pillars found near Roman roads. These, like the Carausius stone, may be milestones or honorific columns. None of this period bear details of distances and destinations though their find-spots show that they undoubtedly stood beside roads. Instead they, like most of their predecessors, simply state imperial titles, in this case those of Constantine and his lineage. Analysis of surviving inscriptions from Roman Britain shows that imperial dedications or other official datable inscriptions peak in the very early third century and thereafter steadily decline until a cessation under Diocletian. Oddly, the so-called milestones steadily increase over the same period, peaking in the mid-third century and then again in the early fourth before disappearing as well. The largest group of all (approximately seventeen percent) belong to the decade 300–10, bearing Constantine I's name as Caesar for the years 306–7. If they were honorific this is difficult

*25   Defences at Caerwent (*Venta Silurum*) in Gwent.*
a. The third-century south wall at Caerwent with its fourth-century bastions, without doubt
the best-preserved Roman urban defences in Britain.
b. The blocked south gate at Caerwent, view from within the town. A drain has been let in to
allow ponding water to escape.

25c. The blocked south gate (detail). The springers of the original arch are quite plain. To the left is the original side of the gate, to the right the blocking stones.

to reconcile with their universal crudity though they evidently advertised the incumbent emperor's name. In Constantine's case the advantages of rapidly disseminating his name are obvious. On the other hand they will have had a practical use in marking out roads in foul weather and of course there is no example of his name on an inscription from any town or fort which would seem the logical place to advertise it.

The survival of the milestones is partly due to remoteness, as with the well-preserved stone from St Hilary, Cornwall (**24**). But others have been located in more densely-populated parts of the province such as one from 3 miles (5km) north of Cambridge. Instances of erased and replaced inscriptions, as well as discarded and buried examples suggests they were normally renewed under fresh regimes, so their survival may be thanks to the practice dying out in Britain after Constantine I. Instead of being replaced, perhaps they stood for decades until they fell over and were buried or were removed for reuse. Only one is attributed to the reign of Constantine II (337–40). Even that depends on the reading, and is in any case carved on the back of one for Constantius I. The evidence points to a policy of road maintenance (though of course the surviving stones cannot be specifically associated with archaeological evidence for new road surfacing) executed in the year 306 and shortly afterwards. Public works, including strengthening town walls (**25a-c**), were an effective means of consolidating power, and also maximizing government control by perhaps being linked with land surveys. For this reason fourth-

26   *One side of the base of a 'Jupiter column' from Cirencester. It states that the column and statue had been restored by Septimius,* rector of Primae Provinciae. *The other surviving panels record that the restoration had been according to the old religion, that Septimius was from Rheims and that the province he governed was* Britannia Prima. *Not earlier than 296. See also* **49**. *Width 410mm. (RIB 103.)*

century road maintenance fell under the control of the regional praetorian prefects and not provincial governors.

Only one of the four provinces of Roman Britain is confirmed on an inscription. Found in Cirencester, it formed the base of an honorific 'Jupiter column' (**26**). The stone carries the name of Lucius Septimius, stated to be *praeses* and *rector* of *Britannia Prima*, making it likely Cirencester was the provincial capital. The most probable date is between the end of Allectus and the Edict of Milan but it is equally possible that it is later as the inscription records a restoration of the column. The most realistic context would be under the pagan revival during the reign of Julian II (360–3) but the stone lacks the information to confirm that and there are no better-dated stylistic parallels.

The London mint remained active until about 325, striking coins for Constantine and his family. New bronze coinage was thereafter supplied by north-western mints like Trier, Arles, and Lyons, but the weights of successive issues were reduced, so a late Constantinian *follis* weighed around a fifth of the Diocletianic equivalent. One series of coins, bearing the *Adventus Aug[usti]* reverse, is thought to represent three dated visits by

27   *Bronze coin of Constantine I struck at London between c. 307–14. The reverse is the
      Adventus Aug[usti] ('the coming of the Emperor') type, recording a visit to London.
      Diameter 22mm.*

Constantine to Britain in the years 307, 312, and 314, based on analysis of the mint-mark
sequences and imperial titles (**27**). The battle against Maxentius in 312 was the climax of
a civil war that required Constantine I to maximize his army. One theory is that his visits,
particularly in 312, were connected with withdrawing troops from the British garrison to
support him. Additional evidence is in Eutropius who states that Constantine visited
Britain, and implies that Constantine had subdued the inhabitants. By 318 he had
assumed the title *Britannicus Maximus*, which suggests a campaign.

   In 337 Constantine died and the Empire was divided between his sons. Constantine II
took the West including Britain, while Constans controlled Africa and the centre, and
Constantius II ruled the East. Naturally this did not last. In 340 Constantine II invaded
Italy but was ambushed and killed by Constans who then took the West. This was the first
major defeat of the western Roman army by other Roman forces. In the winter of 342-3
Constans arrived in Britain with a hundred men. His trip was a surprise, and the historian
Libanius says that at the time Britain was stable. Constantine II may have been so popular
that there was a genuine risk of rebellion. However, when dealing with events in 360
Ammianus Marcellinus compared the failure of Julian II to cross the sea to help the
Britons fight Scots and Picts with Constans' willingness to do just that. The damage by
fire at the three major forts north of Hadrian's Wall, High Rochester, Risingham, and
Bewcastle, is often attributed to this theoretical fighting. But, the idea sometimes
expressed that Constans' visit is recorded on coins depicting him on a galley is incorrect.
The issue belongs to the coinage reform of 346 and later (see Chapter 8) and appeared also
on the coinage of Constantius II. It is a generic standard reverse, depicting the (either)
emperor in a stock heroic pose waving a labarum with the Chi-Rho symbol (**71**). A lead
seal from the Roman wharf at London, bearing Constans' head, is the only rather tenuous
archaeological evidence for the visit.

The revolt of Magnentius

In 350 Magnentius, an army commander under Constans and possibly of British descent, seized the West. He had taken advantage of Constans' decadence and contempt for his soldiers. Constans tried to flee into Spain but was murdered near the Pyrenees. In 351 Magnentius was defeated by Constantius II, leaving him only Gaul and Britain. In 353 he was defeated again and committed suicide. These were the second and third major defeats of the Roman army in the West by other Roman armies. The revolt of Magnentius had serious repercussions for Britain. Constantius II sent Paul, an imperial secretary (*notarius*), to deal with supporters of Magnentius in the British garrison. The implication is that Magnentius' forces had been largely drawn from Britain and that he had enjoyed considerable support, perhaps thanks to a residual memory of Carausius, reinforced by pleasant memories of Constantine II. The wars between Constantine II and Constans, and between Constantius II and Magnentius, had both involved the western Roman army. If troops drawn from Britain were not replaced Britain would be more exposed to barbarian threats. If they were replenished the threat of further rebellions would be restored.

Paul began a terror campaign which masqueraded as a purge of Magnentius' supporters. Charges were trumped up so that innocent men could be imprisoned and ruined. Martinus, the Vicar of Britain, tried to protect people who had had nothing to do with Magnentius. The climax came when Paul threatened to arrest Martinus. Martinus attacked Paul, but failed to kill him and committed suicide on the spot. Some of Paul's victims must have been major landowners but it would be unlikely that the consequences would be identifiable in the villas. What may have been notorious at the time need, in reality, have involved only a few dozen people. The requisition of land and property and its transfer to other owners or the state would be unlikely to result in physical changes. Nevertheless, this is a clear reference to an episode which could have ruined a number of the *honestiores*, perhaps with radical consequences for their estates and even allowing others to become richer by benefiting from the requisitions.

Christianity may have played a role. Once legitimized, the church had accelerated its self-destructive process of schismatic division. Constantius II was an Arian, subscribing to the theology propagated by an Alexandrian priest called Arius (c. 250–336). Arius had believed that Christ was separate from God, and although Christ had been created before time began, was still essentially only human. At the Council of Nicaea in 325 Arius had been excommunicated. Constantius II, who enforced Christianity more actively than his father, wanted to rehabilitate Arianism and find some arrangement which would accommodate all views. His anti-pagan measures (see Chapter 4) may also have provoked opposition in Britain which showed signs of a reactionary interest in paganism.

Being Arian or orthodox (Catholic) was becoming synonymous with the Eastern and Western halves of the Empire respectively. This came to a head in 342 when the Serdica council was called to resolve differences. It only made things worse and Constantius and Constans had to force a compromise. Magnentius exploited the tension, especially when Constantius defeated him at Mursa Major. The bishop of Mursa was an Arian and supported Constantius. Magnentius associated himself with the western orthodox Christians. His coinage included the remarkable, and unique, bronze issue bearing a large Chi-Rho monogram on the reverse and the Alpha and Omega (**28**). The portrait is

28   Bronze coin of Magnentius. The reverse depicts a prominent Christogram (Chi-Rho). Mint of Amiens. Diameter 26mm. (Copyright — The British Museum.)

bareheaded, an important gesture to Christianity because the old traditional imperial laurel crown was associated with Bacchus who used it as a device to clear his head after drinking. Christian writers like Tertullian therefore regarded it as repugnant. Perhaps Paul's activities had more to do with the conflict between Arians and Catholics than is evident from the sources.

Around this time, amongst the opaque personalities of the Romano-British fringe, existed a spectral figure. Unmentioned by contemporary histories, 'Carausius II' is known from a small number of coins usually found amongst hoards of Romano-British copies of coins of Constantius II issued after 353. Sometimes over-struck on earlier coins the most legible examples are clearly versions of the *Fel Temp Reparatio* types but carry poorly-composed legends and very crude portraits. The obverse legends read *Domino Carausio Ces* (or *Censeris*) and the reverse *Domin Conta*. If they represent a short-lived rebellion it was of such insignificance that it escaped the surviving sources. On the other hand they demonstrate that the name of Carausius, which can only have had rebellious associations, continued to circulate in Britain. In the context of the Magnentian rebellion it is tempting to see this as a minor manifestation of a sustained separatist fantasy in Britain.

Taxation and coercion

Taxation, and its ruthless exaction in coin and kind, was essential to Diocletian's administrative hierarchy and army. The imperial budget was managed by the 'Count of the Sacred Largesse', in charge of state handouts. Britain, as a Diocese, had its own 'Receiver of Revenue' (*Rationalis*). The money was administered by the 'Chief Treasurer' (*Praepositus*). Throughout the four provinces officials in the cantonal centres collected the money and sent it to London.

The Roman government paid its officials and soldiers in gold and silver. The coins were too valuable for day-to-day transactions. Some were saved and the rest converted at a money-changer's into bronze, supplied by the state. Apart from what they paid themselves, the money-changers sold the gold and silver coins back to those who needed them to pay taxes. These people brought bronze coins, earned by their businesses, and purchased gold and silver to hand over to the tax-collectors. The money-changers, of course, took cuts either way. Most gold and silver eventually found its way back to the government. Bronze coins ordinarily never went back. To improve the supply of gold Constantine discontinued the *aureus*, minted at a rate of 60 coins to the pound of gold. He replaced it in 312 with the *solidus*, struck at 72 coins to the pound (**plates 24, 25**). As gold was obviously so valuable, and maintained in a cycle of payment from the state and back to the state, the *solidi* were rarely lost and thus extremely rare as finds, other than in hoards.

In the late third century taxation was often levied in kind. Continuous wars made it easier for emperors and rebels to requisition goods as needed. Reforms began under Diocletian when each province was surveyed. Land was counted in *iugera*, equivalent to two-thirds of an acre (0.26ha). Each *iugera* was assessed for tax according to measures of agricultural production called *iuga*. The better the land the more *iuga* it would be worth. The population was assessed on a head-count called *capitatio*. Unfortunately, the ways in which these figures were calculated and measured varied, usually according to local traditions. Women, for example, might be omitted or counted as half a head only. In this way a total value for each villa estate (**29**) or village was produced, based on units of production and numbers of people. Those figures were recorded in the civitas capitals and added together to calculate the total units of production and heads for the region. Taxation thus fell almost exclusively on the countryside.

The next stage was calculating liability per head and agricultural production unit. The Roman government had vast requirements to keep administration, defence, and production operating. These were calculated and the figure divided by the units of agricultural production and heads to produce a liability for each unit. Tax demands trickled down through a hierarchy of officials until they reached clerks in the civitas capitals. They consulted their records to identify local liabilities and issued demands. Potential for corruption was astronomical. Landlords, who came to pay their tenants' taxes, recovered the dues from the tenants in the form of produce and of course could assess it in such a way that they made a profit. A commanding officer in a frontier garrison could inflate assessments of his needs. The taxes demanded varied and, as is the way of variable taxation, they varied upwards. This had not happened before in the Roman world because until then taxes had been fixed. Between the years 324 and 326 the total was said to have doubled.

Collectors, drawn from the *honestiores*, were appointed and were responsible for bringing in the dues and removing them to state warehouses. By definition they were people of influence and property themselves whose prestige and status relied on their possession of capital. These collectors were personally liable for dues owed by bad payers. It follows equally that, should by some lucky chance they were able to exact a surplus, then there was nothing to stop that surplus being pocketed. Being rich and powerful there was a more than sporting chance that some of these individuals 'negotiated' favourable head counts and units of production for their own estates and those of their friends. So the elite of Roman Britain were well-placed to grow wealthier.

The requirements of manning unstable frontiers led to Diocletian substantially enlarging the army. He introduced conscription and obliged the sons of existing soldiers to follow their fathers' careers. As all the administrative officers were counted as soldiers that meant they were condemned to perpetual imperial service. Even financial and mint officials were technically the emperor's slaves or his freedmen. All these servants of the

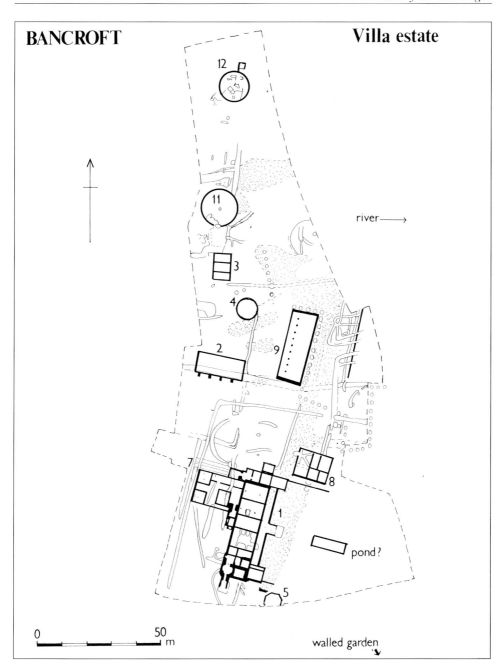

BANCROFT
12
11
3
4
2
9
river——→
7
8
1
pond?
5
0   50 m
walled garden

Villa estate

29   *The villa estate at Bancroft (Bucks). Extensive excavation has uncovered an array of different buildings and tracks near the villa house. In the fourth century each component would have been assessed for taxation. Roundhouses, perhaps for estate workers are at 4, 11, and 12, while 2, 3, 8, and 9 were probably used for agricultural storage. The house itself at 1 overlay an aisled predecessor at 7, and was accompanied by a garden shrine or summerhouse at 5. (After Williams.)*

state were working in what had effectively become compulsory hereditary posts. Serving on town councils was obligatory for those who held the appropriate property qualification. One way out was to work on the imperial service. Of course, it was the better-off who could grease their way into such posts, escaping onerous civitas government positions and all those unpleasant liabilities for taxation shortfalls.

Diocletian created state factories to produce arms and other supplies. Under Constantine the workers in the arms factories were treated as soldiers and by using imperial slaves in the weaving factories all these activities had become hereditary too. One imperial weaving factory in Britain is listed in the *Notitia Dignitatum*. Called a *gynaeceum*, it was run by a procurator at a town unfortunately described only as *Venta* and thus either *Venta Icenorum* (Caistor-by-Norwich) or *Venta Belgarum* (Winchester).

Much of this detail has come down to us from Egyptian papyrii or inscriptions from the Eastern Empire. Assessing its impact on Britain is virtually impossible for we have no written material which would help us measure the effect. We can only work on the assumption that it was eventually instituted more or less as described, across Britain, or that attempts were made to do so. The milestones of the early fourth century may be linked with surveying Britain for this purpose.

4 Towns

Urban development in Britain was the result of government policy and the growth in trade and industry. The effects are clearest in London which, thanks to its unequalled location, grew from nothing into a thriving mercantile centre within a generation of the conquest. Its success, and tribal neutrality, eventually made it an obvious provincial capital. Elsewhere local government towns (the 'civitas capitals') were laid out on or near former tribal centres. By the mid-second century public buildings like the forum and basilica had been designed and built in most major towns (**5**). Meanwhile, smaller unofficial towns were developing largely as a consequence of communications, trade and industry, for example Water Newton in the middle of the Nene Valley pottery industry (**30**).

Ownership of land entitled the wealthy to hold positions of authority in regional government councils. This curial class was able to dominate communities. Such people often owned country houses and townhouses. In the late first century AD Pliny the Younger spent the day on business in Rome and then rode the 16 miles (24km) to Laurentum to spend the night. Three hundred years later Ausonius described how his estate was close enough to Bordeaux for convenience, but not so close that he was affected by the crowds. He added, 'I pass between them, and take pleasure in country and town in turns' (III.i.31-2).

The commercial explosion of the first century levelled off in the early second century. This is most clearly shown in wharfside deposits in London which show a steady decline in the quantities of imported goods. The crowded conditions of the first century gave way gradually to a pattern of more dispersed and better-appointed houses. Some house sites remained occupied, though usually rebuilt, while others became yards or open spaces. By the late fourth century fittings like mosaics were usually being allowed to wear away or were clumsily patched. Some of the open spaces had become filled with a dark soil. Lack of extensive modern excavations in other towns makes it difficult to generalize about this but at Verulamium three blocks adjacent to the forum illustrate a similar pattern.

The only simple explanation for the layers of dark soil in London is that areas had been given over to food production. Given the dominance of the countryside by the villa estates and their resident or absentee landlords, perhaps town dwellers found growing their own food a cheaper option. At Cirencester a house resembling a villa was built in the late fourth century on a virgin site within the walls. With its outbuildings including a possible smithy and finds like a plough coulter, this was probably a town farm perhaps built to take advantage of an urban market no longer adequately served by nearby villa estates (**33**).

Urban housing was not the only sign of change. Romano-British public buildings were built at civic and private expense. Major structures, like the basilica and forum, seem to have required state assistance and action by the community as a whole. In some towns, for

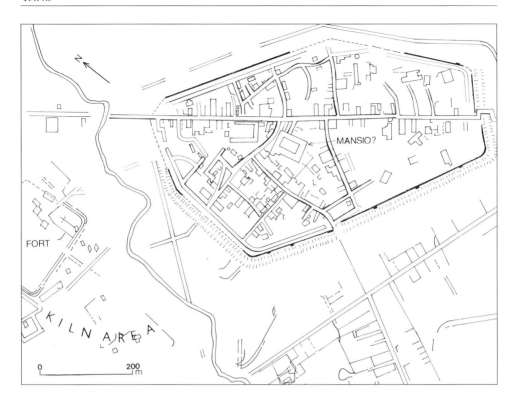

30   Plan of Water Newton (Durobrivae). Unlike Verulamium (5) Durobrivae lacks any
      evidence of formal planning.

example Leicester and Exeter, these major structures were maintained to the end, but elsewhere they were treated as disposable. The Hadrianic basilica in London was unfinished and eventually demolished. Silchester's basilica was used by metalworkers in the late third century. Either it was no longer needed for town government, or it had decayed to a point where there was neither the will nor money to repair it. At Caerwent the fittings which supported the seats in the basilica council chamber were removed around the mid-fourth century, and the rest of the basilica demolished (31). Yet, as little as fifty years before it had been renovated and repaired. The Wroxeter forum and basilica were burnt down by the beginning of the fourth century and were abandoned. At Caistor-by-Norwich the resources did exist to rebuild the forum and basilica in the late third century but on a smaller scale.

    Of course, urban government did not depend on having a basilica (other structures could have been used), but what matters is that what was considered essential in the second century was no longer indispensable. Perhaps in certain areas local government had been parcelled up for so long by the local elite that the basilica had always been a sham. The parallel decline of entertainment establishments was probably connected with the sanctions against urban temples, closely associated with public displays like theatrical

31   *a. The remains of the basilica at Caerwent demolished in the fourth century, looking east.*
     b. Excavations at Caerwent basilica. The worn steps leading from the forum piazza into the
      basilica can be seen in the centre.

performances and games, which began under Constantius II. At Wroxeter the town baths fell into ruin during the fourth century, despite evidence for repairs. At Verulamium the theatre became a public refuse tip. Standing, as it does, close to the forum and across the road from a still-functioning market building the theatre must have presented a dismal aspect. Yet, paradoxically and very unusually, a new house was constructed nearby in the very late fourth century. It belonged to the Roman tradition of well-appointed townhouses in having an internal courtyard and mosaic floors.

Public urban initiatives in the third and fourth centuries seem to have been confined to defences, apart from the rare instances of probable urban churches (see below). Dating defences depends on finds in the detritus swept up into revetments or the later filling of ditches. There are no surviving inscriptions which is an intriguing conundrum in its own right. The general process of providing urban defences seems to have begun in the late second century with earth ramparts which sometimes incorporated existing freestanding monumental gates, like the Balkerne (west) Gate at Colchester. This may have been a province-wide initiative in the face of a military crisis or merely a routine phase in the development and embellishment of towns. There were practical and symbolic advantages in building walls. The movement of goods was more easily controlled (and taxed), and the beginning and end of extra-mural property was more easily defined. Walls also cordoned off zones of status and religious significance. All these functions could have been fulfilled by earthen banks but most were given stone revetments in the third century. Stone walls offered better defences for garrisons and they also looked more imposing (**25**).

During the fourth century stone urban defences were occasionally augmented with additional gates, or reinforcements like bastions and the blocking of gates. This is particularly evident in the defences at Caerwent, the main civitas capital in what is now Gwent in south Wales (**25a-c, plate 3**). Of course, in any one instance, it is not possible to say whether the provision of a stone revetment or blocking of a gate was a matter of convenience or caused by a need for improved security. Equally, the addition of bastions may have been as much a matter of pride as anything else. Nevertheless, such defensive improvements were sometimes built by people who were indifferent to where they obtained materials. These included tombstones, public monuments or the remains of public buildings (**32**). The occasional use of older slabs bearing inscriptions is occasionally helpful in assessing some sort of date. Several of the so-called milestones have been found in the town walls at Bitterne (*Clausentum*) in Hampshire. The latest belong to the reign of the Gallic Emperor Tetricus (270–3); therefore the walls cannot have been built before that date. However, they were found a long time ago and the original context is lost. They may have been used for repairing the walls, rather than building them. The same applies to the milestone of Numerian of 283–4 from Kenchester already mentioned. Of course it is difficult to know whether the reuse of such stones was due to a shortage of suitable building materials in the area or a frantic rush to use whatever was to hand. London is the most conspicuous example of what seems to have been a sort of panic vandalism. The phenomenon is usually attributed to the barbarian invasion of 367 but on the most dubious evidence (see Chapter 7). A century later in a letter to his friend Constantius, Sidonius described damage to Auvergne from Visigoths, but adds that the desolation was as much due to civic dissent as barbarians, characterized by disunity on how to deal with problems:

32   *The fourth-century south-west gate at Lincoln with inverted slab of marble entablature from a*
demolished building (now replaced by a cast).

It's even more to your credit that once you found the city [Auvergne] made desolate as
much by civic disputes as barbarian attacks, you encouraged reconciliation ... they went back,
not only to civic unity but also a common policy, the walls of the city are indebted to you for
the return of the population...
Sidonius (Letters) III.ii.2

It is interesting to see how Sidonius identified the lack of urban organization and harmony
as having been responsible for encouraging people to leave the town rather than a direct
threat of violence. Perhaps in fourth-century Britain a sense of listless resignation and
discord was caused by poor urban leadership in unsettled times.

If the general picture varies one factor does not: there were no prestige public building
projects in the late third and fourth centuries. The private initiative of men like Placidus
at York in 221 was a thing of the past, or at any rate it went unrecorded and is undetectable
in the archaeological record. Yet it is evident from distribution patterns of Romano-British
fine wares of the third and fourth centuries that towns, and the routes between them, still
played an important role in their marketing. Regular finds in central and southern Britain
of North African olive-oil amphorae of the third and fourth centuries, and occasional
examples of fifth-century date, show that inter-province trading contacts endured

throughout the Roman period and beyond even if the levels never matched those of the first two centuries. Such commercial activity, which must have included untraceable perishables like food, is reflected in the small towns, like Water Newton, which had no public buildings to decay. Unlike major towns they relied more on local and indigenous production. They remained at roughly the same size and density as they had two hundred years before. The 'decline' of the major towns was thus relative and primarily connected with their prestige status, and as showcases for public and private munificence.

Constantinian bronze coins of the London mint, closed around 325, circulated on the continent just as contemporary bronze coins from continental mints circulated in Britain. Bronze currency had traditionally circulated locally, but by the fourth century it had become the main form of inter-province cash exchange. It was struck in colossal quantities, officially and unofficially. This means that there is far more to be found compared to most earlier periods. The numbers of coins and the evidence of their movement show that traders were moving between provinces and using them in transactions, reflected in finds of imported wares, and the earlier inscriptions of Placidus the trader. Unfortunately, we cannot distinguish coins lost in use or bulk dumping of periodically demonetized low-value denominations but it seems probable that lively levels of commercial activity were taking place at the same time as urban infrastructure decayed. This is shown in the coin lists for towns like Silchester and Caerwent.

Although reduced building density in major towns suggests that populations had declined, the known urban cemeteries of the fourth century, for example at Cirencester and Colchester, were apparently more extensive than in earlier periods. Many generalizations have been made about this subject in Britain based on minimal areas of excavation and a misunderstanding of the evidence from bones about the deceased's age. It is therefore difficult to form valid conclusions about the Romano-British urban population compared to earlier periods.

The late courtyard house at Verulamium has become almost the 'type-site' for late urban wealth but it is likely that the house was exceptional in a way it would not have been 200 years before in a major town (such houses almost never appear in small towns, and thus the change cannot be observed). Like the Beeches Road farm in Cirencester and the Colliton Park house at Dorchester it was not unique (**33, 88, plate 19**). Such houses suggest that some persons of consequence had opted to stay within the towns and control their interests from there, though of course it is equally possible that these houses belonged to people who spent much of their time on rural estates.

The general cessation of public urban investment must mean that urban administration and an effective system of community investment and shared interests had become more ramshackle and ad-hoc. Consensus government by council members had perhaps led to a gradual transfer of power (in practice, even if not in theory) to a very small number of local magnates or officials, most of whom jealously guarded their wealth on private rural estates. None of this need preclude the existence of large active urban populations, for whom the evidence is ambiguous.

A few inscriptions from Hadrian's Wall are *thought* to date from the fourth century. They appear to represent the record of repair work by working parties sent from various cantonal areas, for example the Durotriges and the Dumnonii. In the context of fourth-

33 *Cirencester Beeches Road 'farmhouse'. Built in the fourth century within the walls of the town on a previously-unused site, it is plain from finds that it was used for farming and light industry.*

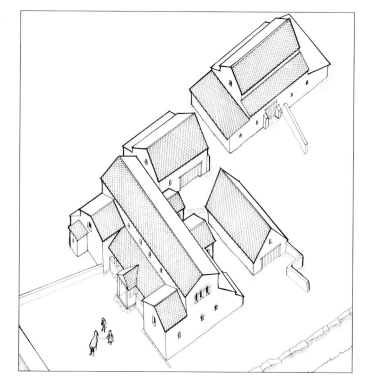

century administration the workers will probably not have been volunteers but the implication is that a diocesan directive went out to the civitas capitals to requisition manpower, perhaps as part of taxation levies. The most likely contexts are repairs to defences under Diocletian, Theodosius, and after Magnus Maximus (see Chapter 7) and they show that local government of a sort was still functioning.

The Church

Civic authority may have begun to take on a new meaning. Christianity was being steadily promoted by the state. Within towns this often meant in practice the appearance of a new urban political and social faction, or even factions, in the form of the resident bishop and his flock as well as rival Christian groups. Constantine I permitted the seizure of temple treasures, though in a spirit of tolerance designed to ease the transition paganism was allowed to continue. Clergy travelled at state expense, and enjoyed exemptions from taxes and other obligations. It became customary for wealthy Christians to leave substantial legacies to the Church. Following major changes in the law in 321, this practice proliferated, helped by priests who 'assisted' people to draw up their wills. In 341 Constantius II outlawed temples within urban boundaries permitting them only to function outside the walls for customary recreational gatherings. Within a few years temples had been banned altogether. It is unlikely that these edicts were comprehensively enforced in Britain not least because they are known to have been enforced in only a piecemeal fashion in other parts of the Empire. Nevertheless, they will have affected the spirit of the times.

The Church was already organized into its own dioceses by the time the Edict of Milan came in 313. In 314 the Council of Arles was held at Constantine's behest to deal with one of the schisms in the early church. Britain sent representatives, recorded in the *Acta* of the Council, including Eborius, Bishop of York, Restitutus, Bishop of London, and Adelphus of somewhere called *Colonia Londenensium*, almost certainly a mistake for Lincoln. A presbyter and a deacon are also recorded. Romano-British bishops attended the Serdica synod in 343 and also the Rimini synod in 360, but neither of the sources specifies the dioceses. Such church officials may have begun to absorb some of the responsibilities for urban government, making traditional institutions and public buildings redundant.

There was a close connection between aristocratic status and the tenure of pagan priesthoods in the towns, reflecting the emperor's traditional role as chief priest, *pontifex maximus*, and his participation in state ritual. Civic priesthoods also involved public ceremonies and provided a way in which the elite could offer their patronage and munificence. The status of Placidus, the trader from Rouen who presented York with an arch and temple, is not clear but he probably held a priesthood.

Constantine I specifically excluded those qualified to serve on councils, their families, and other wealthy people from joining the clergy. This prevented such people from dodging their obligations of public service, and also from paying tax. Of course, they were not prevented from becoming Christians but they were being excluded from maintaining their control of all positions of status. The move also made it possible for Constantine to pack the clergy with people who owed their elevation entirely to him, and not to inherited status. In effect a dual hierarchy was developing: the traditional families were confined to their standard urban duties, while a whole new class of people found themselves enjoying influence, status and privilege of a kind which was steadily usurping more traditional routes to eminence. Not surprisingly this alienated some of the old elite who increasingly began to identify their paganism with the security of the past.

The treasure from Water Newton is the most important example of early Christian plate from the Empire (**plate 4**). It comprises a handled cup, several cups or bowls, jugs, a wine(?) strainer, and more than two dozen silver triangular plaques and a gold disc. The hoard has the most overtly religious tone of any of the major treasures from Roman Britain. Dated on stylistic grounds to the fourth century, but no more precisely, it includes a number of items bearing inscriptions such as *Publianus. Sanctum Altare Tuum Domine Subnixus Honoro* ('I, Publianus, relying on you, honour your holy sanctuary, O Lord'). The two Chi-Rho symbols on this, and several other items including the gold disc, make the material explicitly Christian in spite of the presence of the plaques. The plaque was a pagan convention for recording the fulfilment of a vow to a god, made by someone who had earlier requested a favour and promised a sacrifice or gift in return. One of the plaques bears the statement, *Amicilla votum quo[d] promisit conplevit* ('Amicilla has fulfilled the vow which she promised [she would]') and a Chi-Rho symbol (**34**). Such plaques were normally pinned up outside temples.

The Water Newton plaques suggest that there was a structure, either a church or a house church, in which the plate was stored and outside which the plaques were nailed on display. It need not have been prominent. Icklingham (Suffolk), a much less conspicuous settlement, has produced a Christian baptismal font or tank, and also a small rectangular

34   *Plaques from the Water Newton hoard. Both bear the Chi-Rho symbol, despite being items more commonly associated with pagan activities. The larger (height 157mm) carries no name while the smaller (width 100mm) records the name of Amicilla, who has fulfilled her vow to make the dedication.*

structure which may have been the associated church (**35**). Another example from Brough (Notts), Roman *Crococalana*, is from an area where there is little or no other evidence for Christianity in the Roman period. It bears what may be an earlier form of the Christogram, in this case I X for Iesous X(=Ch)ristos. The inscription on the Water Newton cup naming Publianus includes a reference to a sanctuary. The plaques might even have been made there. This was a Christian community in Britain willing and able to spend money on high-value silver and gold goods, but sufficiently new to have clung on to some pagan habits.

The trend for endowing churches with plate was accelerated by Constantine I who created a custom which eventually produced the extravagant magnificence of the Byzantine churches of the East. The undated inscription from a silver lanx found at Risley Park in Derbyshire records that it was a gift of the Bishop Exuperius to the church of *Bogium* which, like the donor, remains unidentified and may or may not have been in Britain (**78**). Sidonius refers to a friend's gift of a villa estate which was given to an urban church to provide it with income.

> Your gift of the farm at Cuticiacum, so close to the city, is a great addition to this church's
> property ... your inheritance from Nicetius was a reward from heaven for the gift of
> Cuticiacum.'
>   Sidonius to Avitus (Letters) III.i.2

Urban Christian communities sometimes benefited from the philanthropy of the rural rich. This practice began under Constantine, and was another way in which funds, which would otherwise have been available for spending on public works, were diverted. It may have become expedient for some of the urban population to become Christians in order to benefit.

Diverting wealth into Christian communities may not have had a great impact in Britain. Sulpicius Severus, who recorded the attendance of Romano-British bishops at Rimini in 360, explained that three used state funds to cover their expenses thanks to a lack of private support. He does not clarify whether these three were all the Romano-British representatives, or an exceptional minority, but the information suggests that perhaps the Romano-British church was not particularly well-off compared to other provinces. Such evidence as there is for observance of Christianity, for example churches, fonts, and the Lullingstone wall-paintings, shows a bias towards the south and east. This is of limited value but it does seem unlikely that the institution of Christianity was ubiquitous in Roman Britain.

There is no easy way to explain the non-recovery of the Water Newton hoard, especially as it seems to have been the property of a community rather than an individual. The various vessels had been packed into the largest bowl and the handles apparently detached from the handled cup, which makes it likely the legitimate owners had buried it. On the other hand, decaying solder may have caused the handles to come free while so many of the pieces were broken that the treasure must have been buried in a great hurry, perhaps by a thief who later realised it was too identifiable to be easily disposed of. One possible background is Diocletian's edict of 303 ordering the persecution of Christians, the destruction of churches, the surrender of scriptures, and the removal of privileges from upper-class people who were Christians. This was followed by a series of stricter sanctions and the persecution continued until 311. It need not have been the case that these were implemented with any serious effect in Britain, but the prospect of enforcement was probably intimidating.

But it is quite wrong to assume that fear on the part of Christians was necessarily caused by a persecuting pagan state. Sometimes exactly the opposite occasioned violent attacks on Christians. Regardless of legal status, Christianity was extremely unpopular in towns where paganism had a particular hold. This even occurred occasionally in Africa where the Church was well-established. The cities of Sufes, Calama, and Madaura had unrepentantly pagan populations as late as the beginning of the fifth century. In 399 a letter, said to be from St Augustine, was sent to the city government of Sufes concerning the recent massacre of sixty Christians. The murders had followed popular outrage at the destruction of a statue of Hercules in accordance with an edict of Honorius that year which ordered the closure of temples and the destruction of idols. This kind of scenario

35   *a. Lead baptismal font from Icklingham (Suffolk). Diameter 813mm. (Copyright — The*
     British Museum).
     b. Detail of the Icklingham font. The 'Chi-Rho' symbol, representing the first two letters of the
     Greek spelling of 'Christos' are prominent as are the 'A' and 'W', recalling Christ's
     *exhortation, 'I am the Alpha and the Omega' (**Rev. I.8**).*
     (Copyright — The British Museum).

is rarely considered but it is just as plausible a background to the burial of Christian plate at Water Newton. Cirencester's absence from the Arles synod list may be because there was perhaps no Christian diocesan structure there at the time. A piece of wall-plaster from the town bears a word-square of a type generally accepted to be a Christian cryptogram. However, the word-square

ROTAS
OPERA
TENET
AREPO
SATOR

which means 'Arepo the sower is holding the wheels carefully', and can be rearranged to read 'A — Pater Noster — O', is of ambiguous pedigree and far from unequivocal evidence of a Christian group. Even if there was one, it gives us no clues about the presence of a bishop or church.

The spiritual liberalism of the Roman world was initially taxed by Christianity's institutionalized intolerance, something which bewildered Constantine I. The strength of paganism in fourth-century Britain was considerable — it is certainly far more vivid in the archaeological record than Christianity — creating the potential for the kind of violence between rival religions or even between Christian groups which so troubled Augustine. The identification of urban political factions with religious groups might have resulted in disputes which were actually manifestations of local power struggles. Legal privileges enjoyed by the clergy, from which the curial classes were excluded, made them unpopular especially if there was any suggestion of corruption. Christianity could even be powerfully divisive. In 395 Augustine compared the daylight of a service he was participating with the night of the 'gluttonous carnality' being indulged in by the Donatist heretics in an adjacent church. Donatism originated in North Africa and was characterized by an hysterical and zealous veneration for martyrs and rejection of Church authority as polluted by subjectivity and the personal inadequacy of bishops. Either way Augustine felt all the better for the contrast. At Bourges in 470 the death of a bishop led to a local split between supporters of rival successors and was recorded by Sidonius.

> I have come to Bourges, after being summoned by a petition of the population: the appeal was thanks to the collapsing state of the church. The recent loss of the chief priest seems to have been a clarion call to everyone of both persuasions [clerical and lay] to start canvassing for the sacred post. The populace, divided into factions, is alive with animated chatter. Candidates are proposed, or even positively brandished, sometimes by others but often by they themselves.
>
> Sidonius to Agroecius (Letters) VII.v.1

Sidonius goes on to describe that he is only just holding back from suggesting that excitement and greed was at such a fever pitch that most would not hesitate to bribe themselves into the post. This kind of schism could also be provoked by liturgical disputes with violent consequences. This is just as plausible a scenario as pagan persecution for the burial of the Water Newton hoard, especially given its use of the pagan-style plaques which could easily have provoked an outraged and bigoted reaction in another Christian community. Alternatively an anti-pagan pogrom initiated by Christians, of the kind testified elsewhere in the Empire, could have provoked a backlash.

Water Newton has produced no unequivocal evidence for a church of Roman date. Traces of a very large fourth-century hall, up to 50m in width and probably aisled, on Tower Hill in London have been compared to a contemporary cathedral in Milan. Like the Milan cathedral the London hall also had a central well. But confirmation in the form of artefacts or diagnostic features of a church such as an apse have yet to be found, and there were no later churches on the site. At Lincoln an apsidal structure lay under the later church of St Paul-in-the-Bail in the middle of the Roman forum. Of at least sixth-century date, it may represent the location of an earlier church. The better-known 'church' at Silchester which stood beside the forum had many of the diagnostic features of churches including apse, nave, narthex (porch), and transepts. However, the form is not exclusive to churches and this example faces east, exactly the wrong way for a church. There was no corroborating evidence from the building itself or the vicinity. A small tessellated area, once thought to have stood outside the entrance, might have been the base of a baptistery, a common feature, but which provides no confirmation in itself. A recent reinterpretation of the remains has convincingly suggested that the tessellated area was covered by an extension to the narthex. This makes the structure more plausibly a church, but there is not even a Christian graffito from the vicinity.

The Butt Road cemetery at Colchester started as an extra-mural pagan burial ground with bodies oriented north-south, and each usually accompanied by grave goods. In the early fourth century practices at the cemetery altered. These later graves, more than 700 of which were identified, were oriented east-west and the vast majority had no grave goods, both characteristics (but not proof) of Christian burials. However, the association of the graves with a church-like building makes it very likely that they were Christian (**36**). The building, dated on coin evidence to 320–40, was a 24.8m (81ft) long and 7.4 (24ft) wide rectangle with an apse at the east end. Inside, the eastern half of the building had an internal pair of colonnades creating a nave and aisles. It may well have been established as a shrine to a local martyr or saint. The present abbey at St Albans lies close to the eastern defences of Roman Verulamium. It will have grown up around the shrine of the martyr in a Roman graveyard, providing a focal point for a cemetery church which must lie under the abbey. Such was its importance that settlement drifted from the Roman town to the shrine.

Unlike Silchester, Colchester was an important Roman and Celtic religious centre. Prior to the Roman conquest an area nearby, now known as Gosbecks, seems to have formed part of a major sacred site which was developed into a Roman temple zone after 43. Within the Roman city the cult of the deified Claudius was celebrated in one of the very few classical temples known in Britain. Thanks to the building of a Norman castle on its foundations there are few traces of superstructure but some of these have been interpreted as evidence for a major church erected on the temple podium in the fourth century. However, the evidence is restricted to the presence of an eastern apse on the

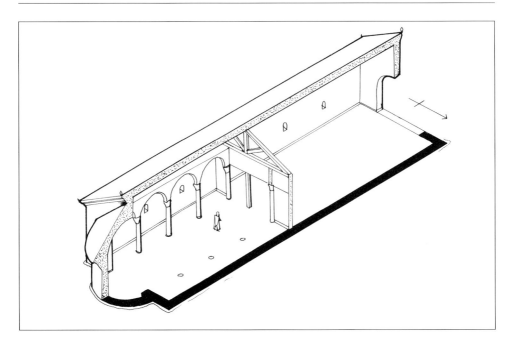

36   Reconstruction drawing of the 'church' at Butt Road, Colchester. Fourth century.

'entrance' and the use of expensive building materials. There is nothing specifically Christian from the site apart from a Chi-Rho scratched onto a storage jar found nearby.

The possibility of Colchester Christians is of less importance than the impression of an active urban community, though of course some of the burials by the Butt Road 'church' may have been those of country people. At Poundbury-by-Dorchester (Dorset) the largely fourth-century cemetery contained a high proportion of east-west burials together with a small number of contemporary mausolea which probably housed the burials of wealthy Christians or senior figures like deacons and bishops. This suggests not only that the cemetery was Christian but that either an urban hierarchy of wealth based on the local Christian community existed, again indicating the presence of some sort of ecclesiastical organization as well as a thriving urban community. On the other hand at Cirencester, where evidence of a Christian community is almost non-existent, cemetery evidence also indicates a flourishing fourth-century community.

In spite of the absence of public and private urban munificence in the fourth century urban communities thus endured. Civic extravagance is the consequence of the wealth, or decisions, of a very small sector of the population. It is therefore possible for a town to exhibit structural decay while at the same time maintaining a substantial population. In exaggerated form this phenomenon is visible in many cities of the developed world today. Likewise, in Roman Britain a small but influential part of the urban community decided to withdraw to the countryside. Some may have found it a convenient way of evading duties imposed on them by Diocletian, but a host of other social, religious, and economic factors could have played a part. As some towns perhaps became increasingly identified with Christianity those who felt that traditional values, symbolized by classical pagan cults and myth, were best enjoyed and revered in rural privacy. Changes in the law may have alienated pagan councillors who saw privilege transferred to an undeserving Christian clergy. They took their wealth away and enjoyed it in a pagan privacy. But committed paganism was not necessarily a qualification for rural withdrawal. Fashion could play a part too. Men like Ausonius, and later Sidonius, both of whom were Christians, belonged to a class of wealthy late-Roman villa owners who extolled the virtues of country living on the grounds of peace and quiet, natural beauty, the opportunities for private reading and reflection. They saw no paradox in their professed religion and their traditional Roman reverence for a mythical bucolic past so eloquently preserved in the works of Virgil.

The Romano-British aristocracy who moved their money away left towns equipped with decaying public buildings but still operating as social and economic organisms. The dramatic effect on the archaeological record may be rather misleading. All that had happened was that the exceptional aspects of first- and second-century urban development, involving the relatively sudden phases of founding and building major towns, had inevitably slowed down. There are dozens of towns in modern Britain which have been through protracted periods of paralysing urban decay yet which still maintain significant active populations. In Roman Britain the change was gradual but in the fourth century major disposable incomes were being spent, by and large, in the countryside and not in the towns.

5 Country

The villas have always been the most easily-identified remnants of the Romano-British countryside. But in recent years archaeologists have focused on other features of villa estates like barns and field boundaries, and beyond, the emergence of villages and the great mass of modest Romano-British farmsteads. Such ordinary houses are now known to dominate the rural record of Roman Britain and were the norm for 95 percent or more of the rural population. But, what really matters for any given period or area is what was unusual or exceptional because this is how the distinctiveness of that period or area is measured.

Modern investigations of pottery distribution have identified an intensification of rural settlement during the fourth century, but predominantly at a very simple level. This means the population as a whole had grown, or people had started to move away from the towns, or that more people were leaving enough behind them to be visible in the archaeological record. No explanation tells us anything about tenure. It would, for example, be consistent with the proliferation of villas and increased exploitation of land where these fourth-century 'peasant' homesteads represent the labourers on huge villa estates.

In the fourth century Romano-British villa buildings increased in total numbers and a few became grandiose. For the Romans a *villa* was a farm, a rural industrial estate, a 'weekend cottage', or a rural property rented to tenants. We use the word to represent a freestanding structure in open countryside which exhibits one or more features to distinguish it from a simple farmstead or hovel. This means a house outside town boundaries with refinements like a corridor, a tessellated floor, perhaps a mosaic, a bath-suite, or wall-plaster. Depending on the time at which the structure was excavated or the aspirations of the local archaeological group responsible even a modestly-appointed rectangular house with a tiled roof might be described as a villa.

Villa types are now classified into a series beginning with the simple rectangular 'cottage' house, divided into rooms. Occasionally, these can be shown to overlie or stand near an earlier native house and in such cases the change to a Roman-type house occurred mostly during the first or second century. The winged-corridor house is defined by the addition of a corridor alongside the main structure and a wing attached to each end (**37**). Some of these 'wings' may actually have been towers, testified on wall-paintings and mosaics from other parts of the Empire (**38**).

The courtyard house was an elaboration of the winged-corridor form where the wings were extended and joined by a fourth wing to create a courtyard (**44**). Some courtyard houses were enlarged by developing the wings again to create additional courtyards. There is much variation and no two are the same. Wings might consist of contiguous rooms, or

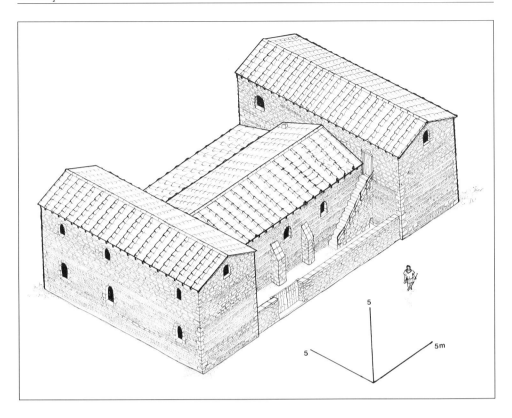

37   *Reconstruction drawing of the winged-corridor house at Redlands Farm, Stanwick
(Northants), as it may have appeared in the fourth century.*

even separate buildings, connected only by a wall. What they all exhibit is the freedom to
grow by sprawling rather than building upwards. This helped minimize the fire risk, and
isolated unpleasant odours from farming or cooking. Although some houses developed
through all these stages, others might be built as a cottage and remain so, or were
constructed as a courtyard house from the beginning. While most elaborate courtyard
villas belong to the fourth century, some existed at earlier dates; similarly, there were many
winged-corridor houses in the fourth century.

'Aisled' villas were rectangular buildings with a nave and aisles, and a roof supported on
posts (**67**). The form was used for churches, mithraic temples, military headquarters and
civic basilicas. Houses of this form, usually fourth-century in date, had an infinite range
of internal room divisions. Some even had protruding corner rooms making them
resemble winged-corridor houses. Evidence for defining the 'villa' is thus based on
physical remains, but does not preclude the possibility that occupants of minor farmsteads
enjoyed other, less tangible, features of romanized life.

Land in conquered provinces was sometimes leased to its original owners. In Britain
this meant permitting the pre-Roman aristocratic families to retain their estates, with the
difference that Roman administration will have introduced definitions of boundary, thus

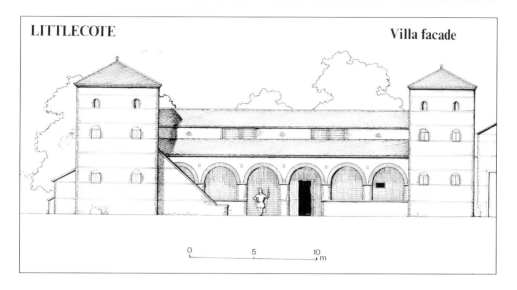

LITTLECOTE   **Villa facade**

0   5   10 m

38   Reconstructed elevation of the house at Littlecote (Wilts) from the fourth-century plan.

consolidating the possessions in perpetuity. These estates could have been huge, and it was quite usual for wealthy people in the Roman world to own more than one property and in more than one province. In a world where natural disasters and climate were completely unpredictable it made perfect sense to disperse investments. In the first century Pliny the Younger debated over whether to buy a neighbouring estate, giving exposure to the same disasters as a good reason not to do so.

> I fear it might be hasty to expose property of this scale to the capriciousness of weather and other day-to-day risks. It might be safer to deal with the risks of fortune by owning property in different places. Not only that, it's pleasant to have a change of place and air, as is journeying between all of one's property.
>
> Pliny to Calvisius Rufus (Letters) III.xix.4

Where the landowner wanted to farm, but had other commitments like political office, the estate was operated by a bailiff (*vilicus*) whose value could be incalculable. Other property was let to tenants (*coloni*) who paid rent. Pliny reduced rents for tenants when the harvests were bad and did his best to visit the estates to calculate dues. During changes of tenancy he was anxious to install new people so that urgent work could be done on the land.

> For the farms, which I possess in this region, earn more than 400,000 sesterces, and I can't put off letting them, not least because new tenants need to be there to take care of the vine pruning which must be done soon. Quite apart from that, the run of poor harvests we have had means that I have to consider putting the rents down, and I can't work out what they should be unless I am there.
>
> Pliny to Trajan (Letters) X.viii.5

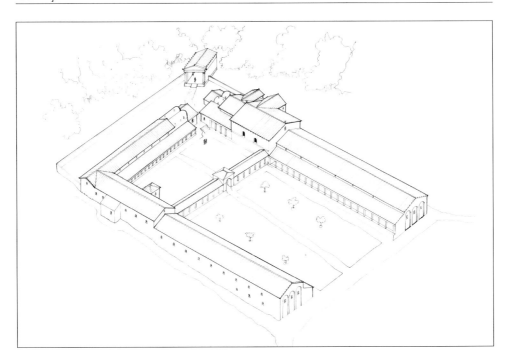

39   a. Reconstructed view of the house at Chedworth as it may have appeared in the fourth
       century. (Based on a view by S. Gibson, but adapted.)
       b. The remains at Chedworth today. Modern cover buildings have been built onto Roman
       wall footings.

39c.   Interior of one of the rooms in the western bath-suite at Chedworth. Although the mosaic floor is well-preserved the wall-plaster has long since come detached, exposing the hypocaust channel made of box tiles.

So, at any one Romano-British villa the occupants may have been tenants of a landowner with colossal possessions and who took a variable interest in what went on. The estate Pliny was considering adding to his portfolio was valued at three million sesterces. At the time this would have been enough to pay the annual wages of more than half a legion. On another occasion he had given a farm worth 100,000 sesterces to his nurse. Other comments provide an insight into the sale of his land by private treaty or at auctions by his freedmen, and the dependence on experienced countrymen able to manage isolated estates.

In the year 404 a Christian heiress called Melania the Younger decided, as many Christians did at the time, to dispose of her estates in Italy, Sicily, North Africa, Spain and (probably) Britain. The information comes from a later 'Life' of Melania which traced her path to sainthood. Such accounts cannot be trusted for detail but the general fact that emerges is of the super-rich controlling land across the Empire. One of Melania's Italian estates was said to contain 62 villages, each with 400 inhabitants. Under imperial law all these people were tied to the estate and their jobs.

Pliny's letters are not automatically relevant to Britain. Legal differences, thanks to time and also local precedent and tradition, may have significantly altered the details of ownership in Britain. But Melania's interests suggest that the substance was probably still true and, if anything, may have become more pronounced. So, some of the Romano-British villas, despite appearing to be individual establishments, were perhaps only parts of colossal concerns and were either occupied by tenants, remained unoccupied apart from household staff, or were even mothballed while the land was still worked. Similarly, a villa estate may have actually belonged to a temple or church, but thanks to the lack of inscriptions either from temples or villas this cannot be demonstrated in any one case.

The vast legal and personal archives which will have recorded all these titles to land, changes and inheritance of ownership have for the most part been destroyed. Lucius Julius Bellicus' involvement in a claim to property in Kent has already been mentioned. A writing tablet, recovered from a well at the villa of Chew Stoke in Avon, is an exceptional instance of survival. Damage and illegibility have made it difficult to interpret exactly but it is clear that it relates to the rights of ownership of what was probably a house (the word is restored in modern readings), and compensation that would be due where possession and occupation had been obstructed by illegal tenants. It is thought, on the basis of the handwriting, to belong to somewhere probably between 175–225. It is unfortunate that it has not been possible to extract more specific information, not least whether it even applied to Chew Stoke. Documents from elsewhere in the Empire refer to house sales involving part-shares in the property concerned, and mortgages or loans. None of these can be specifically applied to Britain but they open up a realm of possibilities which divert us from simplistic assumptions of one family owning, and continuing to own, a villa estate.

Only once does a villa resident appear to name himself for us. The house at Thruxton (Hants) contained a fourth-century mosaic which seems to carry the name of the owner, or at least the tenant. He called himself 'Quintus Natalius Natalinus, [also known as] Bodenius' (**40**). The latter is of uncertain meaning but belongs to a body of Celtic names all starting with *Bod-*. Another example is an outstanding bronze skillet found in the Isle of Ely in Cambridgeshire and now in the British Museum. Entirely Roman in style, with Bacchic imagery, it bears the maker's name 'Boduacus F(ecit)', 'Boduacus made this'. There is no Latin class of words or names which starts with the letters BOD. Natalinus was probably someone whose ancestors were known as Bodenius but who had since adopted a more Roman-sounding name. Boduacus, who may have been a Gaul or a Briton, evidently had Celtic forbears but he had developed his skills to produce Roman goods for a romanized market. If Natalinus was seeking to improve his standing by acquiring a more pretentious name he was not have the first or last. But the importance for us is that it makes it likely his forbears had lived on the site since before the Roman invasion.

Natalinus was probably fairly typical of Romano-British villa owners. It has been suggested that the appearance of fourth-century villa extravagance was due to wealthy Gallic exiles fleeing from barbarians and establishing themselves in Britain. Considering what Ausonius thought of Roman-Britons with cultural aspirations this seems unlikely. When one called Silvius Bonus criticised his poetry he mocked 'Silvius the Good' on the grounds that to be both 'good' and a Briton was impossible. No Briton is testified as holding high office elsewhere in the Roman world. The Romano-British elite seems to have suffered exclusion from the highest echelons of mainstream classical culture. This does not preclude the possibility of absentee landlords like Melania, but the villas in general were almost certainly occupied by people of Romano-British descent and their extended families.

40   *Mosaic from the house at Thruxton (Hants) bearing the name* Quintus Natalius
      Natalinus et Bodeni, *'Quintus Natalius Natalinus and [known by the name of?]
      Bodenius'. Fourth century. (Copyright — The British Museum.)*

Some villas, for example Gayton Thorpe (Norfolk), were made up of two houses
physically separated by only a few metres. At the very least these suggest shared ownership
of the surrounding land, probably by separate branches of the same family. Sometimes this
is discernible within the structure of a single house, as at Spoonley Wood (Gloucs) which
seems to be made up from at least two self-contained but physically contiguous ranges,
based on analysis of doorways through internal walls (**47**).

The absence of villas from parts of southern Britain, for example Salisbury Plain, may
be evidence for the existence of imperial estates. These were lands owned by, and managed
on behalf of, the emperor. At the villa of Combe Down (Avon) an early third-century
inscription is possible evidence that the estate was controlled by a procurators' assistant,
the imperial freedman Naevius. The text only refers to the repair of a building (a
'headquarters', using *principia*, a word with almost exclusively military connotations), and
was in any case reused in a grave some way from the actual house which is presumably of

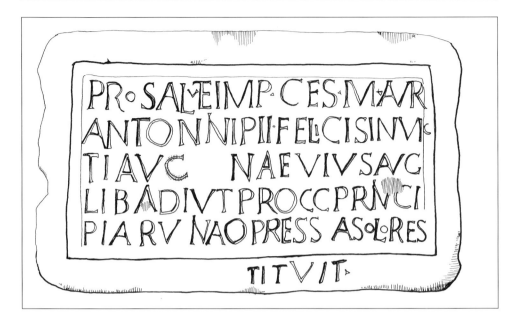

41   *Inscription reused in a grave near the villa at Combe Down at Monkton Combe (Avon),*
      naming Naevius the freedman (lib[ertus]) *and assistant of the procurators* (adiut[or]
      proc[uratorum]) *as responsible for restoring from the ground up* (a solo) *the ruined*
      headquarters (principia ruina). *Probably early third century. Diameter 813mm. (RIB 179).*

later date (**41**). But a lead sealing from the site bears the legend P B R S which is taken to
be an abbreviation for *provinciae Britanniae Superioris* and does suggest that the site was in
official hands at some point after the division of Britain under Severus. However, this is
nearly a century before the time we are concerned with so it may be irrelevant but it raises
the possibility that some imperial estates ended up in private hands in the fourth century.
It might have been expedient for Carausius to buy support by releasing such land.

    The relationship between villas and towns was partly based on the property
qualification for high status. To serve on a town council, and thus influence local
government and the economy, meant owning enough land to fulfil the property
qualification. While land in the immediate vicinity of a town might be conveniently
administered from the town, land more than half a day's walk away needs local
management. The villa was the focal point of any given rural estate. It was here that the
owner (or tenant) had accommodation, storage for agricultural equipment, supplies and
produce, and quarters for staff. The villa house was a manifestation of the status enshrined
in the quantity and quality of the estate.

    Villas thus might be owned by a family which also owned urban property. The family
might own other villas in Britain but given the evidence for the marginalisation of the
Romano-British from prestige status elsewhere it is unlikely that many owned land in
other provinces. The villa may have been in their control for a single generation or for
several generations. Or, it might have been managed by a bailiff on behalf of a temple or

church. And, during the course of a century, any one estate might pass through the hands of different owners which might have left traces in the archaeological record or none at all.

Around a thousand buildings described as 'villas' are known in Britain. They are fairly equally distributed across the Cotswolds and around Bath, and in central, southern, and south-eastern England. Within this general over-view most lie to the east of the Fosse Way apart from a major group to the west between Gloucester and Bath, and there are clusterings along main roads and near towns. The area around Ilchester (Somerset) and the Darenth Valley (Kent) are conspicuous concentrations. Areas notable for a general lack of villas are the Weald of Kent and Sussex, southern Essex, north Norfolk, the wetlands around the Wash, Salisbury Plain and Cranborne Chase, and almost the whole of the 'highland zone' which covers Wales, the extreme south-west and the north. In amongst the villas were numerous simple houses of types which had changed little from before, or during the early part of, the Roman occupation. In areas where there were no, or very few, villas these dwellings constitute almost all the rural settlement. This remained the case throughout the Roman period. Villa concentrations were thus in the most fertile and temperate parts of Britain but not all of those areas had concentrations of villas.

The number of known villas are unlikely to increase much because they are comparatively easy to find unless destroyed or buried under medieval or later houses. The development of the countryside since the eighteenth century, and the manning of the same countryside by antiquarians with time to kill, created the circumstances in which they were likely to turn up. So it is improbable that the surviving distribution differs much from the original, though of course occasional surprises can still occur like the 1997 find of a colossal building at Turkdean (Gloucs). The most consistent feature is a preference for the general vicinity of a town, or a trunk route connecting towns. For legal reasons, villas rarely appear within 5 miles (8km) of a town; in the case of London 15–20 miles (24–32km) would be closer to the truth. Considering its size the lack of villas close to London is surprising, and is almost certainly linked to specific contemporary provisions of which we know nothing except the consequences. Other factors, lost in the mists of untraceable precedent, tradition, and special circumstances, may have contributed to the distribution of villas. Like London some towns, for example Caistor-by-Norwich, Wroxeter, and Exeter, had few villas in their respective vicinities in marked contrast to towns like Cirencester and Winchester.

While towns did not necessarily depend on the proximity of villas, villas did depend on the proximity of towns. Even if a town did not automatically lead to a concentration of villas, where towns were absent so were villas. The Weald of Kent and Sussex is the prime example of a part of south-eastern Britain where there were no towns, and no villas. Only in north Kent were towns strung out along Watling Street from Richborough to London. Accordingly, villas are scattered along the vicinity of the road and its branches along the fertile north-south river valleys of the Medway and Darenth, both tributaries of the Thames. The ability to transport produce, particularly by water, from the villa estates to markets was essential so it is hardly surprising that these and most other villas were close to rivers and roads. Nothing is really known about how this was managed but when discussing the activities of a bailiff Ausonius refers to the use of barges for shipping grain out of villas. Much of Kent seems to have remained primeval forest and, apart from iron-working in the second and third centuries, remained undeveloped in the Roman period. Except for a small number of villas in the coastal area between Dover and Lympne, both Saxon Shore forts, there were virtually no others except in the area around Chichester.

Having said that it does not do to underestimate the mobility of a pre-modern rural population. In an age where mass transportation over colossal distances is taken for granted the paradox is that we have also begun to assume that journeys of minimal length are beyond our abilities without mechanized assistance. As our relative fitness declines that is becoming steadily truer. A nineteenth-century inventor, carpenter, and provincial aesthete from Wales called Thomas Jenkins recorded in his diary for 3 May 1836 that he awoke at 1.15am in order to set out on a 29-mile 11-hour walk from Carmarthen to Haverford West. He spent the day seeing sights and walked back the next day. In the same period it was routine for cattle to be driven from north Wales to London for slaughter and market, taking three weeks in the process. As the conditions of roads were, if anything, better in Roman Britain it seems only sensible to assume that similar activities could, or did, take place.

In the fourth century far more villas developed and did so over a wider area beyond the south and south-east, but many were small, thus reducing the average size compared to the late first and early second century. A few were developed into, or built as, extravagantly-appointed residences on a scale only formerly matched by Fishbourne (Sussex) and Eccles (Kent) in the first century. This trend continued from the very late third century up to the middle of the fourth. Then the number of villas in occupation entered a decline leading to a virtually complete cessation by the middle of the fifth century.

Stagnated development in the towns suggests that surplus wealth was liberated from urban obligations allowing villas to be widely improved. Either as a result of choice or law, or both, there was a change in the spending practices of the rich. The great villa owners could have found a way of creaming off a disproportionate quantity of the province's turnover through the new system instituted by Diocletian. Perhaps the state, through the civitas capitals, disposed of more public land or became powerless to enforce payments of rents from its more powerful tenants. They may have become rich at other peoples' expense rather than as a result of an increase in the province's overall wealth.

Either way, some fourth-century rural landowners found themselves in a position where they could afford a significant increases in expenditure. The state may have granted estates and capital, seized from its opponents, to favoured individuals occupying senior military or civilian posts. The so-called 'Munich Treasure', of uncertain eastern provenance, was buried around the year 324 and includes plate with explicit statements of celebration of imperial rule. One bowl bears an inscription commemorating five years' rule (no mean feat at the time) by Licinius II, celebrated in 322. Similar commemorations appear on some of the other Munich pieces, making it likely they were originally manufactured for the imperial house. One even bears an inscription guaranteeing purity and weight, emphasizing the important role bullion played in storage and movement of wealth. Nevertheless, very little plate bears such explicit inscriptions making it equally possible that uninscribed plate was private property and had been commissioned and purchased as such.

42   *Miniature bronze group of a ploughman with oxen. From Piercebridge (Durham).*
      Height 53mm.

In the circumstances of the fourth century it is possible that Britain offered the potential for relatively undisturbed agricultural exploitation. Northern Gaul had been subjected to a much greater degree of sustained disruption. Improvements in agricultural practice are believed to have taken place in Britain by the fourth century, involving superior metal tools, better techniques of rotation, a broader spread of crops, and new breeds of cattle (**42**). But whether these were causes of increased rural wealth, or effects, is impossible to say. Pollen evidence has been used to argue that deforestation was sustained during the Roman period, thus gradually opening up more and more land for exploitation. If climatic conditions favoured the farming of marginal land then so much the better.

Of course, in the real world, agricultural profits come from shortages or state subsidies not gluts. Private wealth is more likely to have derived from a monopolization of food production than from improvements in technique. The growth in villas represent an increase in individual wealth, relative or actual, the result either of an increase in the gross wealth of a region, or a progressively inequitable distribution of static or declining wealth. Fundamental to either are the specific circumstances affecting a given region or sector of the community. The cotton and rice plantations of the American South in the early nineteenth century exemplify a circumstance in which the coincidence of peculiar conditions of climate, law, demand for a product not easily grown elsewhere, and availability of slave labour, allowed a tiny proportion of the rural population to accumulate colossal individual wealth in a matter of decades. In 1850, of a white population of approximately 6 million, just over 6,000 (or one tenth of one per cent) owned 50 slaves or more. Of the whole, only about 0.35 million owned any slaves at all and constituted the slave-owning middle-class.

The Southern economy depended on the sale of staples to the North and Europe. The most important was cotton, production of which increased four-fold between 1830 and 1860. In 1860 cotton constituted two-thirds of the export trade of the United States. Such vast economic power, concentrated in so few hands, necessarily granted those few hands enormous political and social influence. They defined their world, not only for their contemporaries, but also for us. Wealth accumulated by these people was spent on acquiring more land through favourable marriages, and building ostentatious and pretentious plantation houses filled with fashionable goods from Europe and decorated with paintings of the estate family posing as men of letters with their trophy wives of high style. Little attempt was made to invest the wealth in alternative sources of income or to redistribute it.

This example serves to show what is possible, though it does no more than that, and does not prove that this was how it was in antiquity. But, just as our image of the old South is dominated by the great plantation houses, so our image of fourth-century Roman Britain is dominated by the great villas which appear to represent a not-dissimilar tiny proportion of the population. If the Romano-British economy could be analysed it would be possible to identify special circumstances which had provided opportunities for the few at the expense of the many. However, that economy cannot be analysed in any depth not least because the concept did not exist at the time and thus there is no usable contemporary data, even from other provinces. Instead, the nature of the houses themselves and the surviving contents, examined archaeologically, are the only means by which the incomes, tastes, and priorities of their owners can be assessed.

At this stage the best thing to do is select an example of a Romano-British villa. Bignor is a good place to start because it has been mentioned already and it exists to be seen today. Nothing is known about the owner(s) of Bignor. Taking into account natural features it has been claimed that the likely estate associated with Bignor approximates to 2000 acres (800ha) of good-quality arable land sheltered behind the South Downs. This is of little value because the size of the Bignor household is unknown and the owner may have enjoyed the fruits of other estates further afield. Even though agriculture was normally the primary base of a villa economy, this was not always the case. Occasional evidence of metalworking, brick and tile manufacture, or other industries in the vicinity of other villas suggests that other commercial activities were as, or more, important.

Bignor stands on a south-facing slope of a ridge about half a mile (0.8km) from the main Roman road running between Chichester and London. A spur from the road to the south runs in the direction of the villa. Chichester lies around 9 miles (14.5km) away, the equivalent of perhaps a hard day's round trip by foot and certainly by horse (a perfectly normal activity and distance in a pre-machine age).

Scattered Iron-Age and late-first-century pottery, post-holes and a timber wall-trench, suggest that Bignor was a long-established farmstead which is scarcely surprising given its location. A timber house occupied the site in the late second century but was destroyed by fire. By 240 a rectangular stone house had replaced it. During the next fifty years or more the building was enlarged with a corridor and a pair of wings. This gave the house a definable facade, a feature repeated at many other locations; here the house was altered so that its new front faced the track from the main road. Such embellishments reflected

43 Embellishments at
    Bignor
    a. Plunge-bath at
    Bignor (West Sussex).
    Fourth century.
    b. Column base from
    Bignor. A number of
    these have been found at
    the site and they belie the
    denuded walls of this
    and many other Roman
    villas, making it clear
    that colonnades provided
    architectural pretensions
    as well as shelter from
    the elements.

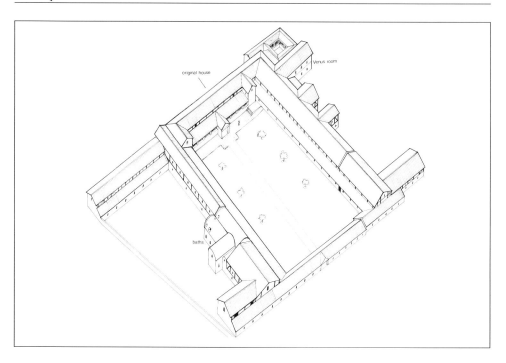

44   *Reconstructed view of the house at Bignor (West Sussex) in its mid-fourth-century heyday.
The winged-corridor house of the third century can be discerned within the west wing.*

practicalities of internal lighting and roofing broad areas. The number of rooms without
an external wall or flanking corridor was always kept to a minimum by maintaining
enlargements as extensions, rather than expansions, of wings.

In the early 300s the original house was retained as the west wing of a larger complex
formed by two, facing, north and south wings. The north wing was continued by two
separate structures of barn-like appearance, and the south wing had a bath suite (**43**). This
effectively tripled the accommodation of the house so the household, perhaps in the form
of an extended family, had probably increased. However, it is equally true that the rich
tend to occupy accommodation in inverse proportion to personal requirements. Only a
single mosaic has been attributed to this phase but as it lies on a lower level others may
have been covered by later floors.

In the mid-fourth century the two barn-like buildings on the north were cleared away
and the north and south wings extended and joined by a new, east, wing. The winged-
corridor house had become a courtyard house with an enclosed rectangular courtyard and
four wings (**44**). In this form it was one of the largest in Britain. The four main wings and
courtyard cover an irregular rectangle of about 7000 square metres. A corridor, facing the
internal courtyard, provided access to all wings. The north wing was augmented by a
number of additional rooms and minor wings which protruded from its north wall.
Within these additional chambers and some of the old north-wing rooms a number of
high-quality polychrome mosaics were laid (**45**, **plates 1, 14**). A small quantity of other

45   *The gladiator and 'Venus' floor at Bignor. From a drawing by Samuel Lysons.*
      *See also **plate 1**. (Copyright — The British Museum.)*

finds provide further evidence for the architectural decoration of the house, such as columns (**43**), while only a gold ring and a bust (now lost) of Fortuna survive from all the personal embellishments and other interior decorations enjoyed by the resident family.

Details of lay-out and size of rooms at Bignor, as with all villas, supply little information about function, a problem which plagues interpretation of any villa plan. One modern survey has attempted a detailed analysis of villas in just this way but the optimism of its author belies the paucity of the material and the general futility of the exercise. However, it can be said that mosaics were normally laid in the most prominent rooms, sometimes heated, while finds of tools suggest utility rooms used for cooking, manufacture, and storage. Assessing function from these or on the basis of doorways, shape and orientation tends to overlook the possibility of altered use over long periods and the fact that by far the greater proportion of the artefacts which would tell us what went on in any one room have not survived.

In the fourth century the potential for enlargements and cosmetic additions enjoyed by a few were such that something very significant must have happened to affect their owners or occupants. Can we devise a scenario to explain Bignor? Yes, but with the proviso that there is no useful information about changes in prices or climate, either of which could affect drastically the operation of a rural estate. Let us suppose that the Bignor owner is a member of the curial class in the canton of the *Regni*, whose capital is at Chichester. The estate guarantees his membership of the cantonal council. The Carausian celebration of Britain's *romanitas* appealed to him but he was not foolish enough to commit himself publicly. Until around the year 300 he and his forbears have enjoyed the tradition of a family home at Bignor and a townhouse in Chichester. Bignor is where they spend the summer and in the winter they repair to Chichester while Bignor remains managed by a bailiff. An alternative might be, on the example of Ausonius, that the senior man lived on the villa estate while his son or sons lived in the town. The family take pride in the knowledge that their ancestors have lived in the vicinity for centuries.

However, our Bignor owner is affected by Diocletian's new laws and the events on the continent. Firstly, his curial duties are now compulsory and his sons are obligated to follow him. Perhaps he resents the privileges awarded to urban Christian clergy under Constantine. Secondly, problems on the continent have had a serious effect on food prices. Merchants who manage to cross the Channel, dodging pirates, are paying high prices for British corn. Government requisition agents make a shortage shorter and prices higher. Profits for the merchants make the risk worthwhile. To make his own life easier our man insists on payment for his produce in silver or gold, and the possession of an accumulating bullion reserve gives him even more power in influencing local market conditions, permits him to buy up adjacent land and allows him access to goods and services denied to others.

Anxious to evade curial duties the Bignor owner uses cash and influence to grease his way into a post which exempts him from tax-collection responsibilities. He may have had access to advance news of state policy. An Egyptian papyrus of about this time carries a remarkable instruction from an official called Dionysius to his bailiff or agent, Apio. Dionysius had wind that the state was planning a devaluation of coinage struck in Italy and tells Apio to convert any estate cash into goods immediately. Anyone else failing to take the same precautions could, overnight, find himself worth a fraction of what he had been the day before. Wealthy people in Britain were just as likely to hold positions where this information was available; perhaps in a remote province they had even more time to act before official policy was promulgated. Poorer people, whose coin reserves were likely to be almost all base metal, could have found themselves ruined without warning, thereby increasing the gap between rich and poor.

Our Bignor man comes to use the townhouse less and less; in any case it is a little too close to the coast for comfort, and he withdraws to Bignor where he has invited his sons (for whom he has purchased positions), and their families, to move in to apartments. His increasing income pays for the structural improvements and extensions to accommodate them. Now enjoying the benefits of a tied workforce our Bignor owner is well-placed to maximize the potential of his estate. He and his cronies in the *Regni* cantonal government compare notes to make sure the system works for them and they parcel up the local economy. Of course they have always done this but present circumstances make it easier to increase profits. They rarely bother any more to go through the motions of dealing with public business in the basilica. They automatically choose to spend money on themselves rather than subsidise the state in the form of funding civic improvements.

That this kind of exodus was not unusual across the Empire is indicated by the laws intended to stop people moving out of their home towns. But in reality, especially in

Britain, the gap between the wording of legislation and its practical enforcement in an ancient Empire was probably far larger than we can properly assess. The wording of the legislation survives because it was enshrined in Roman statutes. Its clarity and purpose are misleading because the practicality of its operation in a remote tribal canton is quite another matter and largely unrecorded. In practice the processes of patronage, cronyism, 'insider dealing' and other corrupt practices were used to the full. There are so many historical parallels that the point seems hardly worth making but post-communist Russia amply illustrates the problems presented to a regime with little practical power. Those people in positions of power with land or bullion are in the best place to enjoy the benefits of their own momentum. Once rolling the momentum has a pace of its own and our Bignor owner, or perhaps now his oldest son, controls local markets, using his personal prestige and contacts to best advantage.

This is a cynical picture which paints the Bignor family in a most unpleasant light. Nevertheless, it shows the various ways in which the most powerful people were able to line their nests. Most of what has been described is testified here and there throughout the Empire. There was also the degree of compliance amongst ordinary people. Ties between villa estates and peasants will have lasted for generations with the Bignor owners having been the local squires for so long that few would have challenged them. Pliny the Younger had been quite able to combine substantial personal wealth with a benign attitude of responsibility, a Roman *noblesse oblige*. Accumulation of wealth need not have created social strains; instead, the creation of nascent feudal estates may have produced microcosms of stability which were jealously guarded. In the face of the ruthless and coercive fourth-century Roman state the protection of a local worthy may have been highly-valued.

There are many cultures in which a few families, privileged by inherited or commercial wealth, were or still are able to run very substantial, sometimes dispersed, estates. This is found in the English seventeenth and eighteenth century, and also in the eastern and southern states of the United States where a variety of colossal, usually slave-owning, estates were possessed by 'old' families whose forbears had received major land-grants from the Crown. Regardless of time or place this dominance was invariably reflected in private estates. The landowner and his family occupied a grandiose establishment characterized by architectural and aesthetic pretensions. The actual house was managed and run by a hierarchy of servants. Beyond, the estate itself would often consist of substantial quantities of farmland worked by the owner's agents who controlled large numbers of agricultural workers occupying houses and villages owned by the family.

Returning to the American South for a comparable example we find Middleton Place, near Charleston in South Carolina, a seventeenth-century estate which was acquired by Henry Middleton through marriage in 1741. Over the next 120 years the estate prospered thanks to the slave trade. Despite a ten-hour journey by river and road to Charleston, the senior Middleton men played influential roles in the War of Independence, national diplomacy, and state government. Substantial private wealth was accumulated from the rice plantation and much of this was spent on the acquisition of European furniture, paintings, and silver. These possessions were displayed in the three separate buildings which made up the family residence. The parallels with the Romano-British villas are obvious.

Identifying the boundaries of a Romano-British villa estate is rarely possible. The natural features around Bignor provide possible limits. At others, such as Ditchley (Oxon) and Winterton (Lincs), circumstantial evidence exists in the form of surviving field-boundaries, footpaths, field systems and natural features. At Stanwick (Northants), a long-term programme of excavation has uncovered a remarkable complex which was centred on a fourth-century villa. Around this building was a series of roundhouses. This seems to have been a villa with its attendant working population accommodated in satellite housing of a type associated with pre-Roman times. The village at Catsgore (Somerset) developed to a state in the fourth century where around a dozen basic farmsteads, with individual enclosures, were clustered together. Here the link to a villa is less obvious but the presence of villas in the region makes it possible Catsgore was inhabited by tenant farmers (**46**). Writing to his friend Domitius, Sidonius refers to his villa estate at *Avitacum* in Gaul almost as if it was a town.

The range of possibilities for any one estate is bewilderingly complex and just as unresolvable. The same applies to the multiplicity of minor Roman settlements which lie within the vicinity of known villas. At Gorhambury (Herts) the villa lies within the smaller of a pair of compounds. In the larger compound a bath and other buildings have been interpreted as facilities for estate workers. A similar situation has been inferred at Gatcombe (Avon) where, despite the absence of a villa (believed destroyed by a railway cutting), a number of small structures interpreted as agricultural, industrial and storage buildings within a walled compound are assumed to represent the centre of the estate as a going financial concern. A hypothetical estate for Gatcombe has been devised, based on natural features, the location of at least eight much more basic, or 'native', occupation sites with a radius of about 3 miles (5km), and the distribution of other villas. The result is a very approximate rectangle, bordered on one side by the river Avon, measuring about 5 miles (8km) by 7 miles (11km) and containing zones suitable for pasture, grazing, and arable.

In high-quality agricultural areas which happen also to be areas of considerable natural beauty fourth-century villas and settlements proliferated. This is best shown in the Cotswolds, criss-crossed by major routes such as Akeman Street from London, and the Fosse Way from Leicester and Lincoln. These routes all converged at Cirencester, the second largest city in Roman Britain. In every respect then the region 'had it made' and this is reflected in the parcelling up of the good land, usually near the roads and river valleys, into separate villa estates and a significant concentration of major villa houses. At Spoonley Wood the large fourth-century house looks west across a valley towards another villa at Wadfield only 1.5 miles (2.4km) away. It might be true that the distribution reflects the ease with which villas are found in accessible and fertile parts of Britain. On the other hand it is equally obvious that stately homes are thinner on the ground in the highlands of Wales and northern Britain.

Spoonley Wood seems to have originated in winged-corridor form, evident within the later plan. This component faced south but the fourth-century additions extended southwards and then westwards to create a west-facing complex (**47**). This took advantage of the spot's natural features of looking west across the valley to Wadfield. It is tempting to see the two houses as being parts of the same estate, especially as both lay close to a road,

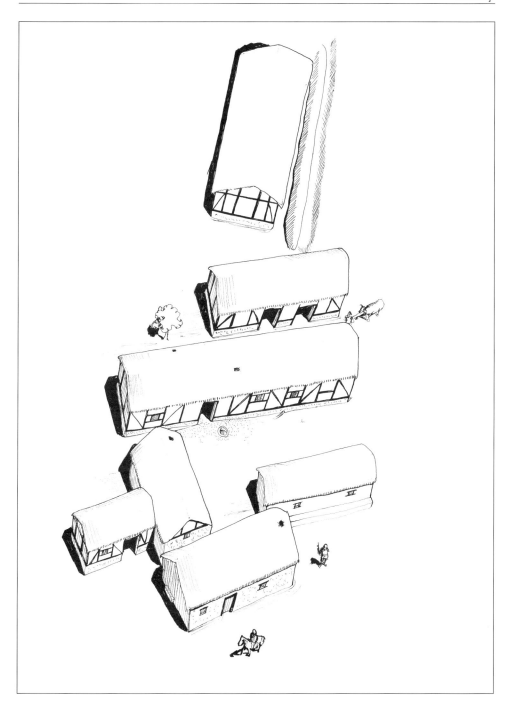

46   *Reconstructed axonometric view of a second- to fourth-century farmstead complex at Catsgore (Somerset) based on the published plan.*

47   *Spoonley Wood as it may have appeared at its height from the west. To the left (north) the winged-corridor house can be seen, now integrated into the extended house.*

perhaps of Roman origin, which runs 3.5 miles (6km) south to the village or small town at Wycomb. Another villa lay only half a mile (0.8km) west of Wycomb.

The recent pinpointing of another major fourth-century house at Turkdean (Gloucs), demolished by the end of the Roman period or shortly afterwards, was accompanied by examination of natural, field, and parish boundaries. This showed the building to lie in the western part of a polygonal area west of, and abutting, the Fosse Way. Not necessarily of Roman origin, the area's boundaries may preserve elements of Roman-period land division. Prior to the identification of the house in 1997, this area was conspicuously devoid of recorded Roman rural settlements apart from one 2 miles (3.2km) to the north-west. This is despite the abundance of Romano-British villas and settlements elsewhere in the Cotswolds. The house, a portion of which was certainly in existence by the second century, had been so systematically demolished that it was undetectable on the surface. Its existence, which might have been surmised given the 'gap', shows that large houses of fourth-century date seem to appear very roughly at distances of 4–8 miles (6.5–13km) apart in the region with a more unpredictable scattering of smaller houses and settlements around them. Only a few miles to the east, for example, a series of villas and villages are strung out along the Windrush Valley, and to the south-west others, including the major house at Chedworth (**39**), lie on the south bank of the river Coln.

These major villas were a world apart from 'ordinary' villas like the house at Barton Court Farm (Oxon). This house, despite origins in the Iron Age, never progressed beyond a range of rooms and a corridor, features which acquired by the fourth century. Its pretensions were confined to an apsidal room, tessellated floors and painted wall-plaster. The occupants were probably limited to members of the immediate family, and a few servants or slaves. Other houses like Bancroft and Rockbourne exhibit many

48   a. *The east bath-suite at Rockbourne (Hants). Although close to the main house the late-third to fourth-century baths were attached by only an external wall. In the fourth century they were supplanted by a refurbished suite which was already integral to the house.*
b. *Hypocaust at Rockbourne at the northern end of the west wing, unusually constructed from curved roof tiles of the **imbrex** form.*

characteristics of the great villas but were clearly more modest establishments. Bancroft (Bucks) is one of a few villas where some of the vicinity has been closely examined, revealing outbuildings, like granaries, and tracks which create an impression of an active farm around a house which never developed beyond winged-corridor form (**29**).

Rockbourne (Hants) is much less well understood because it was excavated intermittently a long time ago. However, the house lies to the north-west of the New Forest in a region where villas are more thinly distributed than they are near the cantonal capital at Winchester to the east. It is also agriculturally less productive than areas to the east and north-west. At its greatest extent, in the fourth century, Rockbourne had grown into three straggling wings around a courtyard but much of this expansion had occurred during the third century. Although it had bathing facilities it had relatively few mosaics, one of which was repaired by someone of outstanding incompetence, for its size and lacked any obvious evidence for architectural pretensions. In Rockbourne's case its location must be connected with its restrained development (**48**).

★★★

The distribution of villas, and in particular the major houses, generally reflects what are still the most agriculturally productive parts of England. Whether the land was selected for aesthetic or economic reasons it is almost invariably the case that the same criteria make the same plots prime land today. First-rank villas of the fourth century are evidence for a Romano-British elite which dominated the control of wealth to a degree which was unprecedented for Britain. It is clear that great villa development took place at the same time as the major towns declined. Lesser villas were owned by people who wished to model their own lives on those of their betters. Before we go on to look at the intellectual and spiritual world of the great villas in more detail we need first to understand the religious and cultural background.

1   *The gladiators from the 'Venus' mosaic at Bignor (West Sussex), discovered in the early nineteenth century. Fourth century.*

2   *The east wall of the Saxon Shore fort at Portchester. Late third century.*

3   *The blocked south gate at Caerwent* (Venta Silurum). *Whether this was for security or because the gate was disused is unknown. The blocking was pierced for drainage suggesting that perhaps the roadway was a quagmire and useless for access.*

4   *The Water Newton Christian hoard. Left to right: bowl dedicated by Publianus (height 115mm), plaque with Chi-Rho motif, jug (height 203mm), two more plaques, and a cantharus cup. Foreground: wine strainer, like the plaques also associated with pagan rituals. (© The British Museum.)*

5   *Stone bust of Mercury from Uley (Gloucs). Lifesize. (© The British Museum.)*

6 *The Romano-Celtic temple at Maiden Castle (Dorset) as it may have appeared in the fourth century. (Painting: the Author.)*

7 *The Romano-Celtic temple at Lamyatt Beacon (Somerset) as it may have appeared in the fourth century. (Painting: the Author.)*

8   Gold items from the Thetford (Norfolk) treasure. (© The British Museum.)

9   Gold crossbow brooch from the Moray Firth (Scotland). Length 790mm. Fourth century.
(© The British Museum.)

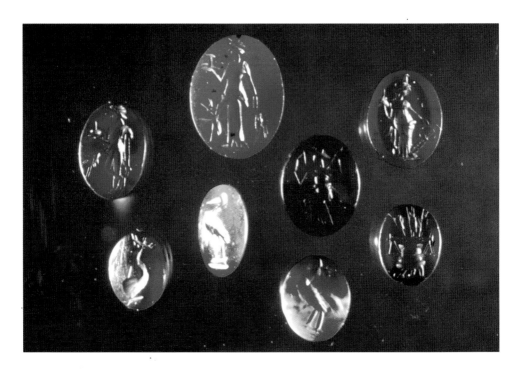

10 *Various intaglios from the Thetford treasure. These stones were already antiques by the time the treasure was buried and were presumably intended for resetting.*
(© The British Museum.)

11 *The Great Dish from the Mildenhall treasure. Diameter 605mm, weight 8.26kg.*
(© The British Museum.)

12 *Figure of Orpheus on a mosaic from the villa at Brading (Isle of Wight).*
(Courtesy of the Oglander Trust).

13 *Littlecote (Wilts). The house and triconch hall as they may have appeared in the mid-fourth*
century. (Painting: the Author.)

14 *Figure of Ganymede on a mosaic from the villa at Bignor (West Sussex).*
(Courtesy of Bignor Roman Villa).

15 *So-called head of Venus on a mosaic from the villa at Bignor (West Sussex). Fourth century.*

16 *Mosaic from the villa at Lullingstone (Kent). In the foreground Europa is abducted by Jupiter as a bull. In the background Bellerophon kills the Chimaera, watched over by the Four Seasons.*

17 The remains of the house at Great Witcombe (Gloucs) looking north. The spring ran from left to right across the middle of the house and down the slope.

18 Hot room (caldarium) in one of the bath suites at Chedworth (Gloucs).

19 Fourth-century townhouse at Colliton Park, Dorchester (Dorset).

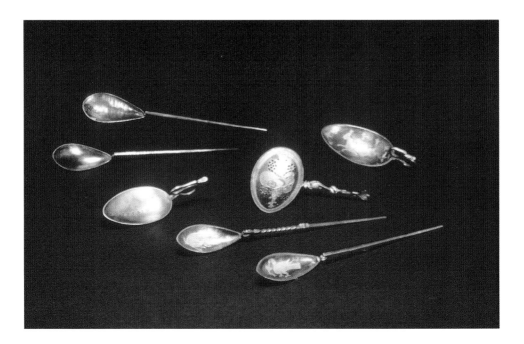

20 *A representative selection of silver spoons, some with gilded decoration, from the Hoxne hoard. The plain spoons bear the inscription* Aur Ursicini, '*[the property] of Aurelius Ursicinus'. The longest are about 200mm in length. (© The British Museum.)*

21 *A group of objects from Hoxne, including a silver pepper pot (see* **plate 22**), *gold body chains, and a bracelet. The bracelet bears the inscription* Utere felix domina Iuliane, '*Lady Juliana, use this with happiness'. (© The British Museum.)*

22 *Silver pepper pot from Hoxne in the form of an unidentified empress, decorated with gilding. Height 103mm. (© The British Museum.)*

23 *Silver tigress from Hoxne, originally a handle from a silver vase. Length 159mm.*
   (© The British Museum.)

24 *Some of the 15,000-odd fourth- and fifth-century silver and gold coins from the Hoxne hoard.*
   (© The British Museum.)

25 Coins

    a. Brass double-sestertius of Postumus (259–68), over-struck on a coin of the first or second century. Obverse only.

    b. Bronze follis of Constantius Chlorus as Caesar. Struck c. 296–305. Reverse depicts the Genius of the People of Rome. Mint of Ticinum (Pavia, Italy).

    c. Bronze coin of Constantine I (307–25). Reverse depicts the Unconquered Sun. At the bottom the letters PLN state that the coin is from the mint of London.

    d. Gold solidus of Valentinian I (364–75). The Hoxne hoard included five such coins. Reverse depicts the Emperor as Restitutor Reipublicae *('Restorer of the Republic'). Mint of Nicomedia (Turkey).*

26 Gold rings from the Thetford hoard. (© The British Museum.)

27 The temple precinct at Bath as it may have appeared in the fourth century. To the left is the spring cover building, now propped up with enormous buttresses devised to combat the effect of the vaulted roof.

6 The Pagan Revival

Constantine's edict of toleration was issued in 313 partly because Christianity was seen as a means of holding the Empire together. Schisms, and other theological disputes, compromised that prospect. So did a sporadic reactionary backlash across the Empire which treated paganism as the authentic foundation of the Roman world. This was precisely what Septimius, governor of *Britannia Prima* had stated on his restored Jupiter column at Cirencester (**26**). A surviving capital from another, or the same, is overtly pagan (**49**). In a time of insecurity the old ways had attractions, thanks to their association with an earlier Empire which had had purpose and destiny. Paganism thus provided a refuge from social fragmentation and declining authority and military power. The resources and will still existed to found new pagan establishments in Britain, mostly in rural areas close to the villa concentrations in the south. A study of temples in Britain has shown that until the mid-third century towns were favoured for new foundations, but thereafter a preference for the countryside took over, no doubt reflecting in part the legal restrictions on temples in urban zones which started to come into force in the 340s.

During the late third and fourth centuries the total number of temples thought to have been in use declined. This was partly offset by the foundation of new temples in rural locations. Perhaps the best example of one of these new shrines is the hill-top complex of temple, baths, and accommodation, dedicated to the Celtic god Nodens at Lydney (Gloucs) (**50**). The combination of an inscription on the temple mosaic almost certainly recording a dream interpreter (not the ludicrously-inappropriate naval official, according to an earlier reading), and other finds associated with healing, make it plain this was a place where Britain's primeval past was merged with the pagan Roman world's love of bucolic settings and recreational pursuits of prophecy, charms, and health. Founded in the late third or early fourth century on an old iron-working site, not far from the large villas in the Cotswolds it was probably dependent on villa clientele, some of whom had perhaps endowed the settlement. It was still possible for more money to be sunk into Lydney when the temple collapsed in the late fourth century, needing redesigning and repair.

At Uley (Gloucs) a pre-Roman religious site remained in use during the Roman period with the erection of a series of new buildings. It was revitalized in the early 300s when a new and unconventional stone temple was built. A pit was used for depositing gifts of coins, much as the sacred spring at Bath had been used. Like Bath, the site has also produced lead curse tablets (nearly 200) in this case often addressed to Mercury. He was also represented by the remains of a life-sized statue (**plate 5**), two altars, and bones of his 'associates', goat, sheep, and fowl. Other new buildings by the temple recall the Nodens complex at Lydney and it seems likely that the shrine was also operating as a commercial and recreational centre. Uley sits across the Bristol Channel only 12 miles (18km) from Lydney and was more accessible to the villas around Cirencester. The Frocester villa is

49 *Bacchus, as depicted on the capital of a Jupiter column from Cirencester. Other figures from Bacchic myth are portrayed on the other sides. It is possible, but no more than, that the Septimius base (see **26**) is from the same column. Fourth century.*

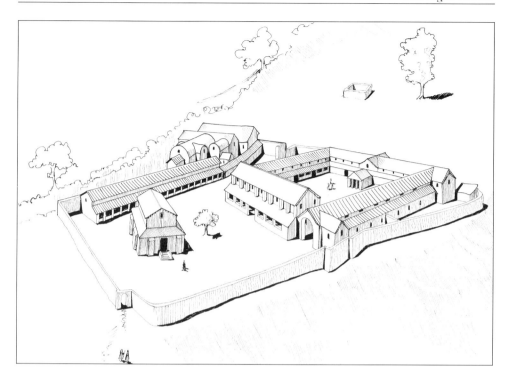

50   *Reconstructed view of the Lydney (Gloucs) Temple of Nodens complex as it may have appeared in the fourth century. (After Wheeler.)*

only 3 miles (5km) away and the major villa at Woodchester only 4 miles (6.5km).

The Iron Age hillfort at Maiden Castle (Dorset) became the location in the fourth century for a modest Romano-Celtic temple (**90, plate 6**) and out-buildings. But the re-use of an ancient hill-fort was shared by Lydney and some other late temples. The most basic reason may have been available land with vaguely traditional cult associations. But Lydney, and to a lesser extent Maiden Castle (where the deity is unknown), had commercial elements. The latter for instance seems to have had a building serving perhaps as a temple 'shop'. Both places would certainly have made pleasant days-out, especially on feast days, and this must have been part of their attraction (**51**). They could have been instituted as primarily commercial ventures, or were provided as self-sufficient philanthropic endeavours by wealthy locals.

The hilltop temple at Lamyatt Beacon (Somerset) was also of Romano-Celtic form, though its entrance had a pair of flanking annexes, and another chamber with a sunken floor was attached to a side wall (**plate 7**). The temple was not built until the late third century and has no obvious association with any one god, Celtic or classical, though a connection with a horned god called Cernunnos is possible. Statuettes of a variety of mainstream Roman gods have also been found here, so it may have been a deliberate attempt to create an all-purpose pagan shrine. The Maiden Castle temple site, for example, produced finds associated with Minerva, Diana, and a Celtic bull god known as Taurus Trigaranus.

51   Temple regalia from Hockwold-cum-Wilton (Norfolk). These bronze head-dresses will have been worn in temple parades and ceremonies. (Copyright — The British Museum.)

A very similar structure to the Lamyatt Beacon temple stood at Brean Down (also in Somerset) and is believed to have been built about 340. This site was also a piece of virgin high ground but in this case occupied the centre of a headland projecting into the Bristol Channel. Its appealing location will almost certainly have made it susceptible to the kind of coastal raiding which is testified in the sources. This would explain why it fell into disuse before the end of the fourth century and at a time when the Lydney temple was being rebuilt.

In contrast to the physical remains of temples, the Thetford (Norfolk) treasure is the clearest evidence for a sect or *collegium* with a serious interest in a revived cult. The hoard, deposited in the late fourth or early fifth century, included 33 silver spoons and other items, of various types, many of which bore inscriptions referring to the god Faunus (**81, plate 8**). On several items his name is paired with others of Celtic origin such as Blotugus ('bringer of corn') and Medugenus ('mead-begotten'). These were presumably members of the sect. That these names are of Celtic type suggests the cult was certainly local to Britain though the names may have been pseudonyms for participants adopting roles. The allusions to Faunus and his lineage on some of the jewellery from the hoard associate even these with the cult. Perhaps the most intriguing connection is the gem depicting a cockerel-headed god known as Iao, and also as Abraxas (a name based on the initials of the Greek names for the days of the week) and Sabaoth (a word for supreme ruler). Both of the latter names are engraved on the gem.

The *absence* of Faunus from the normal run of Romano-British, or other western provincial, cults suggests that he may have been picked as a result of trawling through literature. In other words, a conscious decision was made to extract Faunus from a literary limbo and restore him, almost as if he was a piece of vintage machinery. The period was one of great uncertainty. It seems less surprising, albeit unusual, that a rural god venerated for his prophetic powers in a period of trouble should make an appearance in Roman Britain. The wine-strainer emphasizes the possibility that the spoons and other implements

52   The garden 'shrine' at Chedworth.

found were integral to the practice of a cult which involved eating and drinking to a state of rapturous intoxication.

Referring to a 'cult' at Thetford of course means making an assumption, and it should not be forgotten that much of the Thetford material was made up of what appeared to be a high-class jeweller's stock-in-trade. Faunus may just have been the excuse for an exclusive social club with interests in drunkenness (regarded in antiquity as a medium to achieve higher awareness) and sexual indulgence. But the existence of a cult is plausible. The Orphic floor at Littlecote (Wilts) in its unique triconch hall is a possible candidate for a *collegium* meeting place but there is no way of distinguishing this function from satisfying the eccentric whim of a wealthy individual (**61, 68**). At least the Thetford names supply us with evidence for a small community. Sadly, a catalogue of errors mean that by the time the treasure's existence had been revealed the site had already been built over and thus its true context has been lost forever. Perhaps we should be grateful that we have it at all.

Some of the new, or redeveloped, rural temples lie within a few miles of villas but it is not possible to demonstrate an association though one is likely. Were some 'villa' complexes cult centres and not homes at all? At Chedworth a small garden shrine stands adjacent to the house (**52**). Some villas, like Frampton or Great Witcombe (**62**), have peculiar plans where individual rooms seem to have been of especial importance. Chedworth seems to have rather too many bath facilities to be easily explained (**plate 18**). Yet, none of the mosaics at the sites provide support for the idea of cult centres and the varied nature of religious allusion in the art at villas makes it very difficult to argue conclusively for cults. Unlike Lydney there is no primary evidence for cult activity beyond the usual scattering of household deities. Equally, the bathing facilities may be simply extravagance but there is a possibility that the estate enjoyed additional income from visitors. The site can hardly have been less striking and intimate than it is today. Villa shrines and temples probably had far more in common with chapels built into the stately homes of England and churches on the estates where the livings were in the gift of the landowners.

Pliny the Younger was advised that a temple of Ceres, which stood on his land, needed rebuilding. This was a priority because its anniversary celebrations attracted large numbers of people.

> The soothsayers tell me that I have to rebuild the temple of Ceres on my estate. It needs to be made bigger and improved because it is very old and too small, in view of how crowded it gets on its anniversary on 13 September when huge crowds from the whole region gather there ... I believe it will be an equal gesture of generosity and piety to build the best temple I can and to include porticoes — the former for the goddess and the latter for the public. Therefore please buy me four marble columns, of whatever kind you think appropriate, and marble for improved walls and floors. We also need to commission a statue of the goddess because sheer age has caused several pieces to fall off the old wooden one...
>
> Pliny to Mustius (Letters) IX.xxxix.1ff

Pliny's desires were that his largesse would symbolize his piety while at the same time providing improved amenities for visitors. He seems to express nothing proprietorial about the temple establishment or the cult, regarding his responsibility as an inherited obligation. Pliny's temple was thus an important expression of his personal munificence, but there is no suggestion from him that its presence made his estate into a religious centre. On the other hand it was clearly an attractive feature and his concern for the purchase of appropriate marble columns and fittings represents the aesthetic appeal such an establishment could have. As ever, the world of someone like Pliny may have been very different from that of the Romano-British villa magnates. But there is so much evidence that they modelled themselves on classical culture there is no reason why the appeal of a rural shrine on their land should have passed them by. The relationship between the Woodchester villa owner and the temple at Uley may have been very similar.

Some of the new temples, many of which had novelty locations, may have thrived at the expense of established centres. The temples which suffered were primarily in towns, but it was not unknown for others to fall out of use too. The octagonal temple at Nettleton (Wilts), apparently dedicated to Apollo conflated with a Celtic deity called Cunomaglos, was an elaborate structure which stood at the centre of a small village. Despite evidence for industrial activities, the settlement was probably also associated with servicing the cult and needs of visitors. By the mid-fourth century the temple had collapsed thanks to an inherently unsound design. Nettleton survived, but only as a small pewter-manufacturing and farming centre. Interestingly, the temple had stood very close to the Fosse Way, and thus the major trunk route between Cirencester and Bath.

The roadside settlement of Springhead (Kent), *Vagniacis*, straddled the main route from the coast up to London. At its centre were at least three Romano-Celtic temples within a walled compound. Recorded evidence from the extensive long-term excavations here is rather diffuse but the two main temples seem to have superseded the third some time between 120–50. But, by the mid-fourth century these were derelict and may even have been given over to industrial activity as had happened at Nettleton.

Bath was probably the greatest religious and recreational centre in Roman Britain and Nettleton must have benefited from the passage of traffic en route to the spa (**89**). That Nettleton declined as a cult centre might be evidence for a reduction in regular movements about the province during the middle and later fourth century. Alternatively, it more probably represents a major change in habits reflected across the Empire. As a roadside shrine Nettleton offered convenience but not exclusivity or the spiritual glamour and exclusivity of remote hilltops. The buildings at the heart of Bath's religious and spa complex had started to undergo serious structural problems by the early fourth century. These problems were rectified in the short-term but perhaps Bath was passing out of popularity amongst people searching for some sort of spiritual alternative (**plate 27**). The evidence of the coinage from the spring suggests a tail-off in visits from around the mid-fourth century, dropping to almost nil after 388. This contrasts with the coin finds from conventional town sites.

The Verulamium theatre was an important component of the town's religious zone. But its use as a rubbish dump in the fourth century suggests decline or change in civic religious observance, almost certainly connected with the growth of Christian activity around the shrine of the martyr Alban. At Lincoln, the re-use in a fourth-century gate of a large piece of entablature which is likely to have come from a temple shows that here at least one prestigious classical building had been demolished (**32**). As only a single slab was involved it is very unlikely the temple was dismantled for the express purpose of erecting the gate. It had probably been in ruins for years, thanks to long-term neglect of at least one mainstream urban cult. But at Caerwent, in south Wales, exactly the opposite seems to have happened. Here a new temple, of Romano-Celtic form, was built towards the end of the reign of Constantine and remained in use for much of the rest of the fourth century (**53**). Its proximity to the great villas and also Cirencester, where evidence for Christianity is minimal, makes this perhaps unsurprising.

The rural temple at Harlow (Essex), possibly dedicated to Minerva, was erected in the first century on a site which has produced evidence for its use a ritual centre from the Bronze Age. Despite extensive improvements and rebuilding work in the third century the entire site seems to have become derelict in the fourth. That a place with such long-term religious significance became abandoned suggests that criteria for new pagan centres were different. Harlow lies close to the tribal boundary between the Trinovantes and the Catuvellauni. The Woodeaton (Oxon) temple lay on the other side of Catuvellaunian territory close to its border with the Dobunni.

Such zones are associated with the sites of fairs, a form of annual or episodic social, religious, and commercial gathering which barely exists nowadays but which has a long tradition stretching from prehistory up to early modern times. Springhead and Nettleton must also have benefited not only from the passage of merchants and artisans through the settlements, but also through the consequent commercial activity from markets and fairs. If even this function had become redundant in the fourth century (which may not necessarily have been the case) then we have more evidence for a break in traditional habits and the movement of goods. The remoter new temple sites like Brean Down and Lydney were less likely to act as convenient substitutes, and must have been more reliant

*53   Romano-Celtic temple at Caerwent. The temple was a new foundation in the fourth century
and, considering the evidence for urban paganism at Cirencester (26), suggests the region
may have become a pocket of determined traditionalism.*

on endowments than passing trade. Although Lydney and Uley, for example, were
evidently geared-up to receive large numbers of visitors the decline of urban temples and
the increase of rural temples was probably the consequence of a change in spending habits
by the rich who were increasingly diverting their wealth into personal indulgence.

Early Christianity depended on towns, not least because of the focus on congregational
gatherings, and also because of the laws intended to exclude paganism from towns.
Christianity was not unique in its congregational style but unlike Mithraism, for instance,
it was open to anyone and combined a rejection of the secular with the promise of a
glorious afterlife. This made it popular amongst the urban poor who had the least to lose
and the most to gain. Whether this led to anti-pagan activities in Britain is not really
known. The London mithraeum's destruction in the mid-fourth century, and the careful
burial of its cult statues, is usually attributed to Christian zealotry. Obviously, in a town
the presence of Mithraism would have been particularly conspicuous, making it an
obvious target and a hostile crowd easily gathered. But, similar damage appears to have
been suffered by mithraea in the frontier zone, for example at Carrawburgh and
Rudchester on Hadrian's Wall.

The activities which might have gone on at Thetford were a source of revulsion to some contemporary Christians. A certain amount of undercover activity was needed to maintain cults, regardless of whether there was real spiritual activity or merely debauchery. The usurper Magnentius had rejected the use of a laurel crown on his explicitly Christian coinage, probably because the crown was linked with Bacchic sobering-up. Saint Jerome (c. 345–420), an immensely important early Christian writer and leader who travelled over much of the Empire, had strong views on what wine and strong food could do to a person's self-control. In a letter written in 394, giving advice to a widow on how to live chastely, Jerome reminded her of Christ's advice to avoid drunkenness, and that 'Venus grows cold' (i.e. lust declines) when Bacchus (wine) and Ceres (food) are absent. Although he is not directly concerned with Bacchic or similar cults here Jerome is telling us that from a zealously Christian point of view drinking was automatically associated with paganism, intoxication, and sexual licence (**54**). Earlier, the second-century Christian apologist Tertullian had described Venus and Bacchus as 'the two demons of lust and drunkenness'. Drunkenness, it should be said, was often regarded in antiquity as a higher plain of inspired consciousness. The reverence felt for it is well expressed in Latin poetry (for example by Propertius). Ironically of course many contemporary Christians yearned to achieve similar rapture, but did so through fasting and intensive bouts of prayer which often produced semi-hysterical states.

For the wealthy, and thus better-educated, Christianity in its fully-fledged orthodox sense not infrequently presented an unpalatable challenge to everything which they cherished, although Christ himself was occasionally welcomed into the pantheon of pagan deities and prophets. The Emperor Severus Alexander kept a sanctuary in his palace where he had placed statues of his favourite gods and prophets such as Apollonius the philosopher, Christ, Abraham, and Orpheus, as well as his ancestors. Given the opportunity he worshipped in their presence in the morning, demonstrating the sheer catholicity of private religion in the Roman Empire. Roman paganism was an integral component of Roman civil and military tradition and the tolerance of its adherents, which helped homogenise what would otherwise have been a very disparate collection of cults, made it a potent force. One need only read through the authoritarian, sanctimonious, sexually-repressive, and humourless writings of contemporary Christian leaders like Jerome to appreciate that serious Christianity in the fourth century was unlikely to appeal to everybody.

Paganism was also an essential component of the cultural tradition, particularly with respect to literature and art. The works of Virgil and Ovid in particular were revered as cornerstones of everything that Rome stood for. Jerome agonized over this. He vastly preferred the style in which the great pagan authors had written and deplored the 'harsh and barbarous' language of the Christian prophets. Saint Augustine (354–430) said that although he knew it was futile he was still entranced by Virgil's *Aeneid*.

As committed zealots Jerome and Augustine's dilemma demonstrates the hold pagan tradition had. For others the choice was less traumatic. The poets Ausonius (c. 310–95) and Claudian (c. 370–410/20) seem to have posed as Christians for the sake of political convenience (both were closely involved with the imperial court), but their works are very largely pagan in character. Augustine certainly regarded Claudian as a pagan. In the fifth

54   *Silver Great Dish from the Mildenhall Treasure (diameter: 605mm, weight: 8256g or
      18.2lbs). Also visible are a small platter decorated with a dancing satyr and maenad, a spoon
      with leaf decoration in the bowl, a silver goblet and a silver bowl.
      (Copyright — The British Museum).*

century Sidonius, who became Bishop of Auvergne in 469, referred to Horace and Virgil
whenever it suited him to do so. Others, mostly educated and including many teachers,
simply maintained their paganism which found widespread support in rural areas, which
of course constituted the greater part of the Empire. Here reluctance to change was more
founded on conservatism than any conscious ideology.

Paganism was not, however, excluded from towns. The fourth-century 'Jupiter'
column at Cirencester is an example of a traditional pagan state monument existing at a
time when Christianity was becoming more common in the towns (**26**). Cirencester may
have been a major town where Christianity had had minimal official impact, a
phenomenon known elsewhere in the Empire and even in Africa which was already
largely Christian. Cirencester was the only one of Roman Britain's four principal towns
omitted from the list of churchmen attending the Council of Arles in 314. That

Cirencester also happened to be the centre of a region where the largest numbers of major villas were concentrated may not be unconnected. But in general the pagan withdrawal to the countryside must reflect in part its unpopularity in most urban environments.

The capricious behaviour of emperors made it easier to sustain paganism in the short term. Constantine I had been accommodating, but Constantius II was markedly more hostile. Julian 'the Apostate' had secretly subscribed to pagan literary and philosophical traditions since childhood. After his accession in 361 he lifted the ban (evidently ignored at places like Lydney) on pagan sacrifices. He professed disgust at how court hangers-on had made enormous amounts of money from the requisition of temple property. Official Christianity had not only become tainted by corruption but was also associated with persons of inferior breeding. Julian took measures against priests sitting as judges and drawing up wills, which favoured themselves and the church, on behalf of their hapless clients. Other laws brought the clergy into the tax net.

In Egypt corruption led to the public lynching in 363 of a bishop called Georgius, loathed by pagans and Christians alike for making money out of other people's ruin and acting as an informer. But, the official restoration of paganism did not mean automatic oppression of Christianity. Indeed, Julian invited the various feuding Christian groups to accommodate one another peacefully, knowing that they would not and he could exploit the failure of Christians to act in unison. It was thus comparatively easy for the pagan Julian to appear civilized and tolerant, and to present his Christian opponents as divisive, intolerant, and petty. Pagan practices remained legal until 391 but subsequent measures to outlaw them had to be renewed continually and with very varying degrees of success. Christian regimes were obliged to enforce general intolerance of non-Christian cults, something which was new to the Roman world.

For those disinclined to participate in Christianity either because the theology did not appeal, or because of the exclusivity and the need to take sides in various schismatic disputes, a new brand of rural paganism with its roots in Latin mythology may have proved attractive. Its appeal may have lay in a spiritual alternative, its antique authority, and its secure associations with literature and traditional symbolism. Despite those reactionary yearnings many pagan cults, especially in the north-west, retained a provincial flavour in their imagery, architecture, and associations with local gods.

Evidence for paganism in fourth-century Britain at temples and shrines is for a withdrawal into the countryside. New temples were usually distant from population centres and while not inaccessible, they were certainly not obvious in the way that, say, Nettleton had been. This does not mean that Romano-British pagans were necessarily under threat from torch-bearing urban Christian zealots (they may have been) but it does suggest a preference for private foundations, endowed by wealthy educated members of the upper-classes who revered the classical tradition. The phenomenon occurred all over the Empire but perhaps in Britain it was easier to establish somewhere like the Temple of Nodens, insulated by remoteness and ordinary country people. The impoverished Romano-British bishops at Rimini in 360 may reflect this targeting of funds in a shortage of support for mainstream exclusive Christianity from the wealthy in Britain.

Pagans with money were just as willing to endow new temples as well-to-do Christians were to found churches and hand over all their worldly possessions — not that those with a pagan bent were in any sense averse to accommodating elements of Christianity. There were very polarized points of view in the fourth-century Roman world, not least within the Christian community. But vast numbers of Romans treated Christianity as a new cult to toy with, and borrow from. Orpheus is just one example of another god who offered life after death. Mithraism, an exotic eastern religion popular in the army, offered a similar future, but to men only. For many people Christianity was one of a series of redemption cults, some involving rituals offering the experience of transcendent rapture. The Hinton Christ, for example, could be seen as a pagan manifestation of the Saviour who was added selectively to the pantheon in the best Roman tradition of absolute toleration. There was little problem in incorporating nascent Christian iconography into the whole panoply of Roman mythical imagery, allegory and allusion.

Even one of the Thetford spoons bears a fish which some modern scholars believe represents a Christian element though this is rejected by the specialists who have dealt with that hoard. Fish in fact also have an association with Venus because they had in the myth rescued her during the War of the Titans, while other aquatic scenes appear on mosaics with Orphic or Bacchic references. In the presbytery of St Vitale in Ravenna, built in the sixth century, mosaics including the expressly Christian image of the dove also depict the cantharus (a two-handled vase) and vine leaves, both normal 'Bacchic' images. These only go to show how abstruse these various mythical connections are, and how inappropriate it is to draw dogmatic conclusions from a single symbol when we cannot possibly know all the details of what meant what to whom during this curious period.

The descendants of men like Lunaris had abandoned their traditional tenure of official priesthoods and civic munificence and withdrawn to a more private life. Excluded in the early fourth century from the advantages enjoyed by the new Christian hierarchy, they were condemned to lives of thankless municipal servitude, deprived of the rewards of privilege and the honour of status. The general decline in urban temples indicates less public and state religious activity, an inevitable consequence of the testified requisitioning of temple property and enforced closures. Some of the *honestiores* will have become Christians, especially if it was politically expedient to pose as one. However, there is very little evidence in Britain for the active practising of exclusive Christianity in the fourth century when compared to the number of new rural temples. Legal sanctions against pagan activities were never easily enforced, though they may have provoked the more discreet removal of cult observance to the countryside.

The motivation behind this revived paganism came from the people with money to spend. In Britain, there was perhaps a sense that the world which had made their wealth possible was no longer secure. In our own time similar concerns have promoted a revived interest in 'Celtic' origins and cults, despite a sustained growth in material wealth however inequitably distributed. These activities are occasionally a crude mix of half-remembered, half-imagined, pseudo-lore including Druids, witches, woods, herbs, and chanting in equal measure. But in Roman Britain the most important point for us is that elite paganism was rooted, however crudely, in a sophisticated literary tradition which defined most of late Roman art and creativity and thus it is central to our understanding of the golden age of Roman Britain.

7 Art and culture in the villas

The late-Roman interest in pagan religion and culture found its main expression in the homes and lives of the rich. Much surviving late Romano-British art has literary or mythical associations because these people were at ease with classical imagery and literature. In the English seventeenth century the rich were surrounded by art and literature modelled on the classical and Christian traditions, for example the painting by Simon Verels of Nell Gwynn as Diana. In the Southern states of the USA prior to the Civil War, there were, paradoxically, more institutions of higher education and fewer children's schools than anywhere else in North America. The result was the oddity that more people (essentially the wealthy) could understand Latin in the South than in the rest of the USA, but the proportion of the Southern population which could read and write at all was the lowest in the nation.

For both communities the classical world provided expression in literary, artistic, and architectural forms. These were self-conscious attempts to associate their own societies with what they saw as the greatest age of human history. Within the Roman world, particularly in the third century and afterwards, there was a similar yearning for what already seemed like bygone better times. We tend to perceive the ancient world as an historical whole, overlooking that in the world of late antiquity nostalgia for the age of Augustus was quite common. By then many ordinary people were familiar with the greatest classical poets, particularly Virgil and Ovid. Their works dominated education and provided catch-phrases and allusions, just as Shakespeare does for us. Augustine, writing in his *Confessions* in the fourth century, describes how the *Aeneid* was a fundamental part of his education as it was for every Roman schoolchild. He and Jerome struggled with the love they felt for pagan literature in a Christian environment which refuted it. Ausonius composed a lewd poem, *Cento Nuptialis*, out of phrases from Virgil juxtaposed to create double-entendres and obscenities. The joke would have been wasted had his readership been unfamiliar with Virgil.

Ausonius was a Gaul, born in Bordeaux, who tutored the Emperor Gratian. His life spanned the fourth century and his knowledge of classical literature must have been reflected amongst his educated contemporaries in Gaul and Britain. A century later the Gaulish poet and cleric Sidonius refers in a letter to efforts of a friend of his to encourage important families to abandon the 'scurf' (*squamam*) of the Celtic language and learn the skills of Latin. This, he makes clear, was a defining difference between being a 'Latin' and a 'barbarian'. The context was a later period in Gaul where the influx of barbarians had debased the quality of classical culture, but the aspirations he describes must have been shared by many of the upper-classes in provinces on the fringe of the Empire in the fourth century and before.

The canon of great ancient texts was relatively small, even taking into account that much must be lost. Virgil's *Aeneid* is around 64,000 words long, a little over the length of this book. Moreover, the available literature was dominated at the time by the same few poets and authors who dominate our knowledge of ancient writing. Roman schoolchildren routinely learned the *Aeneid* and Ovid's *Metamorphoses*, even though three centuries or more had passed since their composition. Few teachers would have had complete texts, relying instead on copies of excerpts or their own memories.

For the literate Romano-British classical imagery provided visual resources for allegory, decoration, portraiture, and pretension. It was also a credential of civilisation and their *romanitas*. Mosaic floors depicting scenes from the *Aeneid* would have been instantly recognizable as such. Any joke, or deliberate physical resemblance between the characters and the owners of the house, would have been appreciated. And, in the world of Latin's sophisticated inflections, great play was made of word tricks and hidden meanings. For us, the problem is that it is very difficult to determine whether an image was used because it was attractive and entertaining, or because it had a weightier symbolism. There was a great variation in quality and range. Many mosaic floors and wall-paintings were made up of abstract geometric shapes and forms which may or may not have been symbolic. Either way classical literature and iconography provided the wallpaper which was the backdrop to Romano-British lives. The coinage of Carausius provides the best evidence yet of the mentality which was available to an imaginative usurper in Roman Britain. None of what Carausius did would have been worth a candle if it had meant nothing to the Romano-British. He promised a return to old values and he did so by invoking the literature and religion of classical, not Celtic, values.

By the late third century the Romano-British elite had significant quantities of wealth to spare. The money was available for expenditure on luxuries, which in the ancient world meant goods like literary commissions, jewellery, plate, land, house decorations, and endowments to churches or temples. Expenditure on these was a demonstration of high status and of course it still is today. The Moray Firth crossbow brooch is an excellent example. The so-called crossbow (or 'P-shaped') form was a fourth-century class of brooch with many variations and was mostly manufactured in bronze or silver (**plate 9**). It was a heavy and prominent piece of *equipage* which was used to pin up folds in a cloak. Crossbow brooches were relatively complex to make and were often engraved or inlaid. They were worn by men of, or with pretensions to, high status. The Vandal general Stilicho and his son were depicted on an ivory diptych wearing them.

Some of the rings from Thetford carry visual references to Faunus, suggesting that the jeweller was either an important member of the cult or was in the process of working on material associated either with the cult or belonging to people who had an interest in Faunus. These pieces were of very high intrinsic value and made more so by their outstanding quality. They appear to represent pieces belonging to a single commission from someone who was both wealthy, educated and refined, and, while extremely rare now, it is unlikely that they were at the time.

The Mildenhall Treasure is dominated by the silver Great Dish (**plate 11**), one of the largest pieces of surviving Roman plate. With it were two much smaller platters, a dish, six flanged bowls, a bowl with a cover, a fluted bowl with handles, two goblets, five ladle-bowls, and nine spoons, several of which bear Christian inscriptions (**54**). Apart from the Christian references on the spoons the decoration of the Mildenhall Treasure is pagan. The centrepiece of the Great Dish, for example, is the head of a sea-god. Around him two concentric circles contain parading figures, the outer group of which includes Bacchus in his triumph over Hercules.

Bacchic iconography was a traditional decoration for Roman feasting plate going back to the first century BC. But Bacchus and his associates like Faunus were also linked with cult practices which included intoxication. In a letter to the pagan grammarian Maximus in the year 390 Augustine expressed his disdain for Bacchic ritual, secrecy, and restriction to initiates. He was revolted by the way in which it destroyed reason by provoking a state of frenzy acted out in public by persons of status. That these practices were regarded with such disgust by committed Christians makes the inclusion of spoons bearing Christian references in the Mildenhall assemblage curious. Either the Mildenhall owners belonged to that class of Roman which took pleasure in different types of decoration, or the hoard was made up from different sources and thus perhaps was buried by a thief.

Unlike the Thetford material, the Mildenhall plate seems to have been accumulated from different places and times and was probably chosen for its decorative appeal. In the first century AD Pliny the Elder discussed silver plate and its importance as a mark of changing fashions. For example, such and such a factory becomes popular, only to be supplanted by another, and so on. He talks of patterns, such as the 'Delos', much as our own antique books discuss the 'Willow' pattern on eighteenth-century china. But he makes no reference to the symbolism of the iconography; instead the subject matter of the decoration is described as a more important indicator of the craftsman responsible, for example 'goblets engraved with Centaurs and Bacchants by Acragas', whose hunting scenes were also highly-prized.

> Fashions in silver plate go through the most extraordinary changes, thanks to the whims of people's tastes, and not one single style of workmanship stays popular long. On one occasion Firnian plate is sought after, then Clodian, on another occasion Gratian ... It's remarkable that gold-working has failed to make a celebrity of anyone whereas celebrated silversmiths are numerous...
>
> Pliny the Elder (Natural History) XXXIII.139ff, 154

The concept of renowned trademarks and their association with the elite is one which is very familiar to us. Perhaps the Mildenhall Great Dish was prized because it was a work by a prestigious silversmith, distinguished by his trademark use of decoration, and the symbolism of no importance. This is a useful, and plausible, alternative interpretation. According to Pliny the desire to display sheer quantity 'used for decorating sideboards' had become an obsession. Roman Britain three hundred years later may have been different in some respects but it seems unlikely that seeking to own the most and the best could have taken second place to symbolic details of iconography. However, by

55   Flagon from the Appleshaw (Hants) pewter hoard. As a Chi-Rho was incised on a dish from the hoard, and a fish on another, the plate may have been used in a house church. Fourth century. (Copyright — The British Museum.)

comparison with Pliny's tales of 100lb+ dishes, the Mildenhall Treasure would have been fairly inconsequential and is a salutary reminder that we have a minuscule proportion of what there once was.

For the less well-to-do the market provided a variety of acceptable substitutes. Pewter, when new and highly-polished, bears a close resemblance to silver and was more easily manufactured, due to its softness and low melting point. The availability of lead and tin, the two components of pewter, in Britain made pewter an obvious Romano-British industry. Nettleton (Wilts) became a pewter-manufacturing settlement in the fourth century. A square pewter dish from Icklingham (Suffolk), with its beaded rim decoration, is very similar to a silver version from Mileham (Norfolk), and shows that prestige styles could be made of inferior materials when the market required. A hoard of pewter with Christian associations from Appleshaw (Hants) was found relatively close to the site of a Roman house and was probably the household plate (**55**).

However unusual the gold jewellery from the Thetford and Hoxne hoards is, there are many similar items known in bronze which were obviously cheaper. It is easy to forget when looking at a deeply-patinated dark-green bronze ring or bracelet that when new and polished it will have resembled gold. Crossbow brooches survive in an enormous variety of types, almost all made of bronze. These pieces were the ancient equivalent of down-market products for mass consumption, and tells us much about the existence of an elite, and the setting of fashions.

For the rich there were other spending options which did not produce durable artefacts, such as fine fabrics, exotic foods, libraries, the patronage of poets and artists, and live entertainments. At a few villas, such as Frocester (Gloucs), careful excavation has shown that time and money was spent on developing formal gardens. In most societies it is the rich who support the creative. This is an equally good way to sponsor vulgarity and extravagance; but, people such as Van Dyck and Mozart were only in a position to do what they did because a wealthy and privileged caste of their respective societies liked their work, and would pay for it.

Our perception of the seventeenth and eighteenth centuries in Europe is very largely defined by the surviving products of the creativity of these and other individuals. London in the late 1700s is, for us, the London of Handel, Hogarth, and Johnson (amongst others) because their creativity not only characterizes the period for us but their works also serve as the media through which we experience the period. This is not misguided because what we are looking at is what was exceptional about those years. That hordes of peasants slaved thanklessly for generations in the fields is something we ought to know and understand but a slaving peasant in the 1700s in England is not really any more useful a defining factor of his age than a slaving Romano-British farmer is for his. If it was, then no age would be distinguishable from another and is something that the modern archaeologist striding across the arid plains of models and statistics sometimes forgets.

With so many shortcomings in our evidence for what was unusual in Roman Britain we have to rely on what there is. The physical evidence of the great houses is perhaps the most important because there are enough of them to see patterns. Treasure hoards are always unique and rarely have parallels of any form; also, their lack of association with settlements makes it very difficult for us to place them in any kind of context. The houses and their floors survive for the simple reason that no-one can roll up a mosaic and carry it away, apart from antiquarians and archaeologists. Despite the damage done by weathering, agriculture, and animals, enough survives to tell us that the fourth century in parts of Roman Britain was the age of villas and master mosaicists.

Unlike gold and silver objects, which could have been made anywhere in the Empire, mosaics were manufactured in Britain by people living in Britain. The mosaicists could have come from elsewhere in the Empire, or were working to designs devised by the owner using pattern books or copies of great and famous (now long lost) paintings. This reflects the mobility of the rich in the Roman Empire, or at least the mobility of their tastes. The bordered squares containing scenes from myth, for example Achilles on Skyros, in the hexagonal floor at Keynsham (Avon) look exactly like paintings. In the seventeenth century needlework on travelling caskets often depicted scenes from classical myth, themselves modelled on widely-circulating engravings which were in turn based on

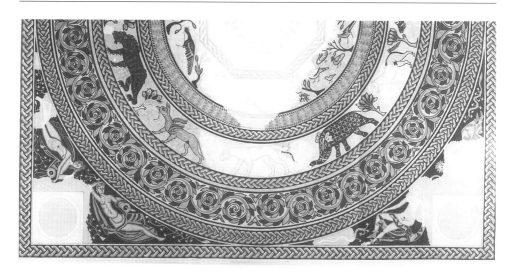

56   *Part of the great Orphic floor at Woodchester (Gloucs). Note the spaces for column bases. The floor remains buried but a fragment is on display at the British Museum. From a drawing by Samuel Lysons.*
    (Copyright — The British Museum.)

contemporary paintings. An excellent example is the 'Faith and Hope' casket of about 1670, now in the Whitworth Art Gallery in Manchester. Its scenes from Ovid have been traced back to the work of Marten de Vos (1532–1603) but it is unlikely that the accomplished needlewoman was aware of this.

It is impossible to tell whether the various allusions were of spiritual importance to the owners, reflected a more opaque interest in religion and philosophy, or were selected because they were pretty. That they were fashionable is plain from the range of quality available ranging from the outstanding Woodchester Orpheus floor (**56**) to crude provincial representations of classical deities. Topics could be abstract, realistic, or mythical (literary and religious). The latter was the most flexible because it combined reality with allegory. It provided opportunities for portraiture, display of knowledge, word games, and also a backdrop to religious ritual.

Mosaics excited little comment amongst ancient authors, even if Julius Caesar's love of luxury was said to have caused him to transport portable mosaics around on campaign. In the first century BC Varro mentioned that a villa might be noteworthy for its painted walls, woodwork, and impressive mosaic floors. Pliny the Elder, a century later, was exclusively concerned with technique and skill, making no comment about their importance as prestige items or their symbolism. For Vitruvius the only thing to worry about was polishing a mosaic floor. This partly reflected that, when these men wrote, figured and polychrome mosaics were unusual. It was not until the second century and later that the black-and-white geometric patterns of the first century gave way to a freer range of motifs and colours.

116

57   *Marble figure of Bacchus from*
      Spoonley Wood (Gloucs).
      Found in a Roman grave near
      to the villa and presumably
      once part of garden or house
      decoration. Height 400mm.
      Either mid-second or fourth
      century.
      (Copyright — The
      British Museum.)

Mosaic floors, however, must have been expensive because they took time to lay, and required specialists. If they had been cheap everyone would have had one. Everyone in Roman Britain did not have mosaics and it is plain from some of the mid-sized villas that if only one could be afforded then one it would be, because one mosaic was better than no mosaic at all. As wealthy people in our own time have several cars, bathrooms, and other conveniences, so the wealthy Romano-British had several mosaics, many of which were on the bigger size too, laid in the most prominent rooms of their houses.

Were the conditions of survival other than they are, the bigger villas would also produce evidence for libraries, more and bigger furniture, more extravagant wall-paintings, and more 'household' than 'farmyard' slaves. Other examples of villa decorations are extant but rare. The head of Fortuna (now lost) from the baths at Bignor, the Spoonley Wood Bacchus and the Diana from Woodchester are scarce examples of house and garden statuary (**57, 58**). Pieces like this are extremely difficult to date and in the past the late

117

58   *Marble figure of Diana Luna from*
      Woodchester (Gloucs). Height
      500mm.
      (Copyright — The British
      Museum.)

second or fourth century have been suggested. The contexts, and the increasing evidence for classical tastes in the later Roman period, make the fourth century more likely. Substantial masonry components like columns, and carved slabs, are even more difficult to date but probably belong to the most elaborate, normally later, period of a house's life. A large column capital survives at Wadfield (Gloucs), and many other villas have produced sections of more modest columns and other stone fittings such as balustrades (**59**) and decorative finials from roofs. Furniture normally survives only in the form of shale table legs and slabs from possible sideboards. At Rockbourne large fragments of a Chilmark (Somerset) stone table or sideboard, decorated with a scallop, a rosette, and triangles set in semi-circles, have been recovered.

Sometimes houses were extended to accommodate improved decorative fittings or facilities such as bath houses, for example at Lufton (**69**). At Lullingstone the modest house was constrained from serious expansion by its location between a river and a

59   Section of stone balustrade from the house at Chedworth (Gloucs).

hillside. Nonetheless, the west range of rooms was pierced during the fourth century to create a room laid with a mosaic floor which protruded from the old west wall in an apse (**plate 16**).

The Orphic mosaics are in several fourth-century houses near Cirencester, for example Barton Farm, Woodchester (**56**), and Withington (**60**), though there are others such as Brading on the Isle of Wight (**plate 12**) and Horkstow (Lincs). There is no parallel for this group elsewhere in the Empire, and it is attributed to one of two theoretical mosaic 'schools' in the town, the other being distinguished by its use of geometric forms. Such a 'school' was probably based on a single craftsman and a few selected pupils. Similarities between the Woodchester and Barton Farm floors are thought to indicate that the same man was responsible, though it is just as possible that one man copied another's work to produce something in the same, popular, style. Orpheus, an important figure in the late-Roman canon of redemption gods, was linked with the Sun, the mystery god Iao, and Bacchus (whose rites he was believed to have devised), and had powers of prophecy. According to the second-century geographer Pausanias, Orpheus was believed to have uncovered divine mysteries, rituals which purified evil, cures for illness, and devices to counter curses placed on people by the gods.

Tracking these connections in classical literature reveals a mass of abstruse information, and it is difficult to be certain what is symbolic of what. This is partly due to the fragmentary nature of some sources, and the unavoidable compression or simplification of themes and scenes to make them fit into a floor, but it is also probable that Romano-

60   *Orphic floor from Withington (Gloucs). Orpheus, accompanied by the usual hound, is
      encircled by running animals. Neptune overlooks the scene in a panel now on display at the
      British Museum and beyond is a hunt. From a drawing by Samuel Lysons.
      (Copyright — The British Museum.)*

British villa owners and their mosaicists were little wiser than we are. They would have
been in good company. In the first century BC a perplexed Cicero described the various
contradictory myths concerning the same gods, listing for example the different
parentages of the Olympian gods, and the paradox that the Sun's name *Sol*, 'alone', meant
his oneness but that there were numerous other sun gods like the Egyptian one. This, and
the evidence for how gauche and unsophisticated the Romano-British appeared to the
Roman world, means that contradictions or confusions found in the iconography of
Romano-British mosaic floors should not surprise us.

The Orphic floor at Woodchester was probably displayed as an example of *tour de force*
mosaic craft in its own time (**56**). In its fourth-century form the villa had been developed
into a series of wings surrounding three courtyards. In total area the villa was no bigger
than many other examples but an exceptionally large central room covering 225 square
metres, designed around the stunning Orphic floor, was laid out in the north wing. The
figure of the god playing his lyre (now lost) was surrounded by a series of concentric
circles containing his animal associates, together with geometric elements. This was a
stock Orphic theme but it also resolved the problem of the way the floor 'faced' which
affected floors composed of rectangular or square panels. The plain outer area, and the
bases of four columns, show that there was probably a gallery from which to view the floor
which, at ground level, would have been difficult to appreciate or even lay. This idea has
been rejected in one modern survey on the grounds that a dignitary at floor level would

61   *Orphic floor from Littlecote (Wilts). The picture omits a dog or fox restored to the relaid floor.
      From a drawing by Samuel Lysons. (Copyright — The British Museum.)*

have disallowed lesser individuals to view him and his floor from above. This curiously narrow judgement makes all sorts of assumptions about who had access, the symbolism of the floor and its function, quite apart from overlooking the possibility that the owner might care to view his own mosaic and share it with his equals from an advantageous position. The fact that it, and all other mosaics, are invariably illustrated from overhead in our own time, rather than obliquely from eye-height only serves to emphasise the point.

The Littlecote (Wilts) example in its freestanding triconch hall is marginally more likely to have had active religious connotations but the physical attraction of its setting is no less evident than at Woodchester. At Brading a series of unusual mosaics depict Orpheus (**plate 12**), scenes associated with Bacchic myth (for example satyrs and maenads, Lycurgus attacking Ambrosia, Ceres and Triptolemus), and Perseus and Andromeda. Another floor includes a panel depicting a human figure with a cock's head confronting two griffins outside a small building set on a hill. The figure is sometimes identified as Iao, also represented on a gem from Thetford under his other names Abraxas and Sabaoth. However, it has been suggested (much more convincingly) that this floor depicts scenes based on African circus themes using fantastic animals, and perhaps employing plays on the Latin for cock, *gallus*, also a common name and perhaps referring to an arena hero, *venator*, called the same. The Horkstow Orphic floor included a scene of chariot races and scenes from the myths associated with Achilles.

Interpretation of Brading is complicated by the damaged areas, but the owner was clearly well-versed in literature and myth or aspired to be. The house is close to the river Yar and Bembridge harbour, making it likely that he had a high social or political profile on the mainland, reflected in the sophistication of the mosaic themes. Perhaps the most interesting figure is the astronomer, symbolic of reason, on a rectangular panel dividing the two main floors. It may be an all-purpose depiction of a philosopher based (however indirectly) on images with origins in fourth-century-BC Athens as Roger Ling has suggested. Or it may be a portrait of the owner, a man of means who was fascinated by the Universe and the science of its workings as well as its mythical origin, posing as one of his philosopher heroes.

Orphic mosaics were evidently popular amongst some Romano-British villa owners. They were integral to the architectural and artistic pretensions of the age, perhaps the equivalent kudos of owning a Salvador Dali or a Picasso. They may represent the existence of a local fad, though whether the fad was for the worship of Orpheus or the attraction of the motifs cannot be identified. If demand had increased then the cost would have risen, and thus the prestige of ownership through exclusivity was enhanced. In the context of an elite community the exclusivity of owning a prestigious mosaic may have mattered far more than the iconographic content.

At some fourth-century villas where architecture and locations seem significant, the mosaics appear to be relatively neutral. At Great Witcombe (Gloucs) the H-shaped house sits astride a stream on a steep north-east slope with spectacular views (**62, plate 17**). Springs were important in pagan religion and in Britain's pre-Roman past they had been venerated. So the idea that Great Witcombe was associated with a water cult is not, on the face of it, implausible. However, it does not do to over-egg the 'ritual' potential of natural phenomena. At his villa of *Avitacum* in Gaul, Sidonius proudly boasted to friends of the

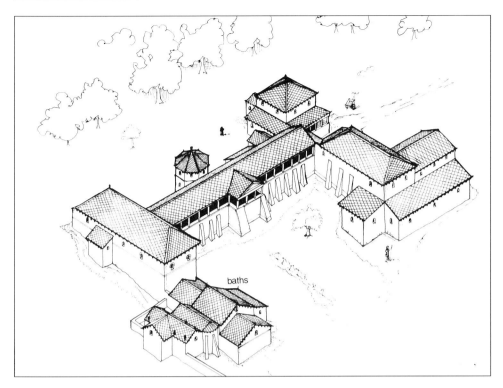

62   *a. Reconstruction drawing of the house at Great Witcombe (Gloucs) as it may have appeared in the fourth century.*
b. Room at Great Witcombe in the centre of the south wing. It stood next to the baths and had its own font and niches in the wall. Perhaps a shrine, it may have been devised as an appealing and secluded part of the house, recalling Sidonius' pride in the entertaining qualities of his own home.

63   *Mosaic from the villa at Stonesfield (Oxon) depicting, amongst the geometric motifs, a mask of Neptune in a border encircling an image of Bacchus and a panther. The floor was found in 1712 and was one of the earliest to be discussed in detail. (Copyright — The British Museum.)*

pleasures of drinks chilled in the cold water of the spring incorporated into the house.

> Then, should a chilled drink be brought to you from that most widely-acclaimed spring, you shall see in the cups, at the moment they are filled to capacity, traces and fragments of frozen mist...
>
> Sidonius to Domitius (Letters) II.ii.12

As a Christian, pagan associations would have been of little concern to Sidonius. But the reference is a reminder that water's primary value is practical and that refrigeration would have been an important benefit of building a villa on or by a spring.

The recorded mosaics at Great Witcombe include two which are skilfully-executed conventional geometric designs. In one a cantharus forms the centrepiece. The device is normally associated with Bacchus but it also appears on later Christian mosaics at Ravenna. A third floor depicts a marine scene including fishes and sea monsters. Again, this has potential Bacchic associations but as the room concerned formed part of the bath-suite it is far more likely it was purely decorative. At the Stonesfield (Oxon) villa Bacchus riding a panther was the centrepiece of one of two roundels within a pair of square zones set in a rectangular pavement. Neptune appears beside Bacchus but perhaps 95 per cent of the floor, as recorded, was geometric (**63**). Other floors in the house were entirely geometric. No temple in Roman Britain has produced a mosaic which is comparable to anything found in the villas, or which has any imagery associated with the cult. A marine

64   *The head of Christ from the Hinton St Mary (Dorset) floor.*
      (Copyright — The British Museum.)

scene was featured on a mosaic, now lost, from the Temple of Nodens at Lydney had nothing obvious to do with the cult even though an inscription on the floor is now recognized to have referred to dream interpretation.

There is no evidence for actual mosaic workshops in Cirencester, or any other town. However, just as villa distribution shows that access to towns was linked with size and wealth so the distribution of villa mosaics makes it likely that towns were the hubs for luxury industries, even though the expenditure and enjoyment of wealth was firmly located in the countryside. The Dorchester (Dorset) Durobrivan 'school' is credited with mosaics in the area featuring mythological and marine scenes. These include the floors from Frampton and Hinton St Mary (both Dorset) which carry unequivocal references to Christianity side-by-side with pagan elements.

The mosaic at Hinton St Mary has what seems to be a portrait of Christ in its central roundel. The superimposition of the figure on a Chi-Rho symbol makes it likely that Christ is meant. The Hinton Christ is sometimes said to resemble images of Christ in the surviving domes of Byzantine churches in the East (**64**). It is earlier than any other known example and also lacks a beard, an important feature of Eastern Christs. The only real resemblance is the depiction of a full-frontal face, a style which had already appeared on some third- and fourth-century coin issues. The irregularity of the partially-invisible Chi-Rho suggests the mosaicist was copying a drawing or pattern without actually understanding what it was he was reproducing.

Other components of the Hinton floor, such as the figure in each corner (identified variously as the Four Winds, the Four Seasons or the Four Evangelists), stags, and trees all recall components of the Orphic or other floors. This does not mean that the floor has to be Christian or pagan; rather it symbolizes an interest in the iconography of creation myth which may have been experimental or even casual.

An adjacent panel depicts Bellerophon and the Chimaera, a kind of all-purpose image of strength triumphing over evil. The scene appears not infrequently in association with Christian imagery but was already a well-established theme for mosaics. The floor at Frampton (Dorset), probably laid by the same mosaicist, carries a Chi-Rho, but also includes (probably) Bellerophon killing the Chimaera, and various motifs associated with Bacchus such as dolphins, a two-handled cup, and a panther in the guise of which Bacchus once appeared as well as a mask of Neptune and a frieze of dolphins (**65**). Panthers, and the two-handled cup, also appear on the Orphic floor at Littlecote.

Thanks to their Christian elements the Frampton and Hinton floors have carried a disproportionate sense of their significance into our own times. In the fourth century Christian art was at an early stage of development. Consequently, most themes and images were adapted from traditional iconography and myth. This must have contributed to Bishop Exuperius' gift of the Risley Park lanx (**78**, and see Chapter 3) and its pagan subject matter. The lanx cannot be precisely dated, not least because it was cast with figures engaged in a woodland hunt, a commonplace theme on Roman decorative tableware. Not only does a similar scene appear on the Mildenhall plate but such activities also appear on Gaulish samian pottery of the first and second centuries. A small temple, of pagan form, even appears in the scene. The likelihood is that Exuperius acquired the lanx at some stage, presumably in the fourth century after the legitimization of the church, and donated it to the *Bogium* establishment either for practical use in ritual or as an endowment. He, and the church, may or may not have been Romano-British. But when the lanx came to Britain Exuperius may have been entirely unknown to its then owner.

Much mosaic imagery amounts to variations on the infinite range of combinations. The Hinton Christ could as easily have been replaced with Medusa, thus instantly altering our interpretations of all the other elements. In this way the 'Evangelists' would become the Four Seasons. An interesting perspective on the Chimaera in the Christian mind comes from another letter of Jerome; he likened his bitter theological enemy (whom he called 'the Grunter') to the Chimaera, quoting a line from Lucretius. On one hand this might be taken as clear evidence that Christians equated the Chimaera with the Devil; on the other, and probably more accurately, it shows how the image was a generally popular symbol of defeated evil, not exclusive to Christians.

Perhaps these floors tell us more about the literary and aesthetic tastes (or pretensions) of their owners than anything more profound. This does not deny the symbolism of the components, but does suggest that it might not have been quite as deliberate as sometimes assumed. If it was, we might expect to find similar material in temples and churches. Frampton is also one of a few mosaics which carry Latin inscriptions. These are possibly useful evidence for literary associations, already present in the iconography. At Lullingstone the image of Europa on the bull is accompanied by a couplet (**plate 16**),

65   *The 'Christian' mosaic from Frampton (Dorset). Apart from the Chi-Rho nothing else on the floor is unequivocally Christian. From a drawing by Samuel Lysons. The Latin inscriptions on the floor, damaged and incomplete, refer to Neptune but proceed to acclaim the greater power of Cupid.*
(Copyright — The British Museum.)

INVIDA SI TA[URI] VIDISSET IUNO NATATUS
IUSTIUS AEOLIAS ISSET ADUSQUE DOMOS

The line, not a known piece of Latin literature, means, 'If jealous Juno had seen thus the swimming of the bull she would, with greater justice, have repaired to the halls of Aeolus'. It refers to an episode in the first book of Virgil's *Aeneid* but it has been argued that the lines emulate Ovid's use of language. One might think of an allusion to a scene in *Macbeth*, but wittily composed in the style of Milton. Whoever composed the Lullingstone lines knew his literature but had recreated it in his own form. This may have been the owner, or it may have been a Romano-British poet, popular at the time and perhaps a client of the villa owner, but completely unknown to us. The floor at Frampton, reputedly destroyed by the mid-1850s, bore a damaged inscription partly restored to read

[NEC MU]NUS PERFICIS ULLUM
[SI DI]GNARE CUPIDO

NEPTUNI VERTEX REG(I)MEN
SORTITI MOBILE VENTIS

SCUL(P)TUM CUI C(A)ERULA ES(T)
DELFINIS CINCTA DUO[BUS]

This can been translated as, '...if you decide it's appropriate Cupid, [then] you perform no service. The wind-blown domain is drawn by lot by the bust of Neptune, whose image is flanked by a pair of dolphins.' Translation into English, however freely, destroys the original rhythm of the Latin composition but the meaning, which remains in some doubt, still seems peculiarly abstruse and pointless. Unlike Lullingstone there is no obvious association with known texts though the wording still evidently relates to the imagery on the floor. The possibility exists that perhaps some additional meaning is concealed within the lettering though omitted characters suggest it was laid by someone who misread or misconstrued written instructions. If that was the case then any significant hidden meaning would have been rendered pointless. At Lullingstone at least one name has been extracted from the couplet by extracting letters at fixed intervals to produce 'Avitus'. But perhaps the purpose was simply to entertain. Sidonius smugly recounted how the walls of his bath-house were decorated with lines of verse to amuse and interest his visitors rather than presenting them with paintings of 'immoral' nude figures. He announced to his friend Domitius that,

> In brief, nothing will be found drawn on those spaces which it would be more appropriate to avoid looking at. Only a couple of lines of verse will make a guest pause and read. Such things strike a balance, because they can be read without boredom even if they do nothing to make one long to read them again.
> Sidonius (Letters) II.ii.7

That single comment calls into question the amount of scholarly time expended on analysing a mosaic couplet which might very well have been glanced at once by a visitor and instantly forgotten for ever more. There is no modern parallel though perhaps embroidered and framed moral exhortations and slogans produced by Victorians have some similarities. If the 'joke', assuming there was one, at Frampton or even Lullingstone is lost on us then that should be no surprise. As we know nothing about the owner then any pun on or allusion to his name, interests, habits or amusements contained within the lines is going to pass us by.

As a habit lettering on mosaics was certainly far from popular. No other mosaics from Britain, and there are plenty of them, had anything similar. The handful of other recorded inscriptions are little more than labels or slogans. A pair from Woodchester seem to say *Bonum eventum, bene c(olite)*, translated as 'Worship Bonus Eventus daily'. In everyday English they might better be given as, 'bless your lucky stars every time you wake up'. Even in spite of the millennia separating us from the commissioner of those lines and his or her tastes it seems fantastically banal. Sidonius would certainly have been right that anyone troubling to read it in the first place would undoubtedly have never bothered to do so again. At Winterton a pair of months, June and December, seem to have been labelled and at Aldborough the Greek characters for 'Helicon' serve probably as a simple label for the inhabitants of Helicon, otherwise known as the Muses. Lettering on a floor at Rudston seems to be purely descriptive, for example *Taurus Omicida*, the 'Man-eating Bull', on a panel depicting a bull. Even the lines on the mosaic from the temple of Nodens at Lydney seem to be purely functional in recording in mosaic form a dedication which might conventionally have been recorded on an altar.

The insignificance of mosaic inscriptions aside Pliny the Younger, Ausonius, and Sidonius amongst others, all tell us that cultivated Romans spent time in their libraries reading and composing prose and poetry. To each other they sent copies of their new books, or even exchanged ideas and drafts while texts were being composed. Most had in mind emulating the work of great poets like Homer and Virgil. Pliny wrote to his friend Caninius Rufus to commend the latter's plans to write a poem about Trajan's Dacian campaigns. Much of the letter concerns itself with the poetic techniques required to deal with the subject matter, especially the problem of barbarian names,

> In any case, if Homer is allowed to shorten, lengthen, and twist the adaptable syllables of Greek in order to make it fit the smoothness of his verse, why should you be prevented from similar freedoms ..?
>
> ... send me every part as you complete it, or even better send each part unpolished in its first draft as it is first composed.
>
> Pliny (Letters) VIII.4 (see also VII.25)

Sidonius describes the home of his friend Consentius as beautifully located, with symmetrical architecture and landscaped surroundings, and a library where Consentius spent much of his time writing poetry.

> [Your] home stands high, and its walls arranged with skill to create architecture with a symmetry beyond question ... apart from having a full larder and large quantities of furniture, it is packed with copious stores of books, amongst which you put in as much work as you do in the fields, so that it's difficult to work out whether your estate or brain has been better cultivated.
>
> As I recall it was here that you produced with diligent labour ... iambics that bowled along, ingenious elegiacs, and well-formed hendecasyllables ... Through these verses it was inevitable you would win increasing acceptance amongst those of your own time and increasing fame in later ages...
>
> Sidonius (Letters) VIII.iv.2-3

These men aspired to accomplishments in style where the manipulation of words into metrical verse, or the treatment of a subject in stylized Latin prose, was treated as a highly-respectable achievement. The compositions were read at private readings, in public, or anxiously solicited in correspondence. None of this of course guarantees that they were virtuoso performers or writers; what matters is that the activity was a credential of status and society.

There is, incidentally, no suggestion that the fruits of their literary labours be recorded on their walls and floors. But perhaps some mosaics served as attractive backdrops to such readings. The iconography of some is vastly more allusive than the small number of mosaic inscriptions. The series of floors at Low Ham (Somerset) are amongst the most expressly literary from Roman Britain. Five scenes from the *Aeneid* depict Aeneas' encounter with Dido. Aeneas also probably appears at Frampton (Dorset), plucking the golden bough, in a scene formerly identified as 'Mars' plucking a leaf from a tree. Some of the stories were far older. The tale of Lycurgus and Dionysus (Bacchus) is recounted in Book Six of the *Iliad*, followed shortly afterwards in the same text by the story of Bellerophon and the Chimaera. Many of these widely-known standard myths, for example that of Apollo and Marsyas depicted in the poorly-executed floor at Lenthay Green (Dorset), or Jupiter abducting Ganymede at Bignor in a vastly superior example (**plate 14**), were also described in Ovid's *Metamorphoses*.

The books and manuscripts in Consentius' library were the sort of material which will have provided sources for house decorations, not just from the texts but also from the illuminations which will have embellished some of them. Literary evidence for the existence of villa libraries, which of course do not survive, supports an idea that a text of Virgil now in the Vatican is actually of a fourth-century Romano-British origin; this is on the evidence of illuminations which resemble images found on some mosaics. The scenes and figures would have provided useful templates with the faces of the owner and his family perhaps being substituted. These were handy opportunities to have the lady of the house depicted in a suitable mythological or classical pose. The so-called 'Venus' on a Bignor mosaic (**45, plate 15**) is almost certainly a portrait of the lady of the house posing as a goddess, just as Charles II's mistresses posed as classical deities. It is likely that many other mythical figures on mosaic floors were modelled on the villa families. The evidence of the archive at Vindolanda, from the waterlogged remains of a single bonfire on a single fort on the northern frontier, shows that that the absence of evidence for manuscripts is a normal deficiency of the process of survival and not because they were never there. The Vindolanda archive, dating to about 95-105, even contains a line from the *Aeneid* in what was probably a handwriting exercise.

Unlike all the other villas, Lullingstone provides evidence for worship of a very particular sort which is beyond reasonable doubt. The house was adapted around the year 380 to include rooms decorated with an unambiguous series of Christian images. Not only did two of the panels include a prominent Chi-Rho symbol but another depicts a series of individuals with arms outstretched, a standard early posture of Christian prayer (**66**). These were probably portraits of the group members. Other very fragmentary remains may have depicted scenes from the Bible. There are no stray elements of Orphic or Bacchic imagery or other associations.

130

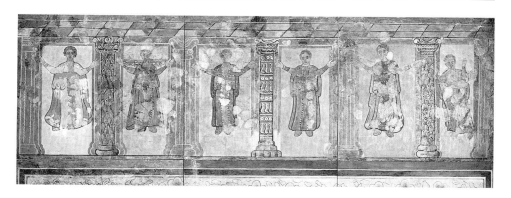

66   a. *The Christians at prayer from Lullingstone (Kent). The panel has been restored from hundreds of fragments of fallen wall-plaster and there is consequently some debate about the exact postures. Late fourth century.*
(Copyright — The British Museum.)
b. *The northern end of the house at Lullingstone, looking east. The collapsed Christian wall paintings were found shattered in the fill of the rooms to the left. It may therefore be assumed that they once stood in an upper storey.*

The Lullingstone paintings are unparalleled in Britain. House churches, which are mentioned in the New Testament, provided convenient venues for small Christian communities and, in this instance, show that the wealthy Romano-British rural elite was not exclusively committed to a pagan revival. By the end of the fourth century the legal sanctions against even rural paganism had increased, and elsewhere Christian groups were actively destroying rural shrines. So it is possible that the fourth-century pagan revival had begun to dwindle as Christianity permeated every level of society. The crisis of Pelagianism and the Church's mission to Britain in the 420s to resolve the heresy points to a Romano-British Christianity which had endured as the only semblance of structure left. Nevertheless, Lullingstone is exceptional and no evidence of Christian worship survived there, so whether the paintings actually decorated a functioning chapel, or were just symbolic of the owners' interests, will remain unknown.

Wall-painting at other villas might provide clues about function, if only it existed in large areas. No Romano-British villa has walls surviving to significant heights, apart from cellars. Wall-paintings are thus always fragmentary and only dedicated restoration work produces results. This is largely a modern skill and few villas, many of which were 'excavated' in the eighteenth and nineteenth centuries, have benefited. Occasional fragments reveal that the literary content was probably similar to the very limited quantity known on mosaic floors. At Otford, near Lullingstone, a fragment of wall-plaster bears the words *bina manu l[ato]*, a line from the *Aeneid*. Whether this phrase, 'two spears in hand', was part of a longer quote associated with a scene from the Aeneid (though a surviving figure armed with a spear makes it likely) or simply a slogan to entertain a visitor is unknown. Other examples largely consist of no more than a handful of meaningless letters from the middle of words, the rest of which have long since crumbled into dust. The house at Colliton Park, Dorchester, yielded a graffito reading *paternus scripsit*, 'Paternus wrote this'. That may have amused a visitor but would probably have irritated the owner. There is little then in the surviving wording on wall plaster to suggest much in the way of a pagan revival. What exists though shows an undoubted latinity about the writers. They wrote in Latin or in some cases Greek, had Latin names and used Latin words.

The appearance of apparent mythical figures is more common but it is rarely possible to say precisely who or what is being depicted. A very damaged fourth-century wall at Kingscote (Gloucs) may show Achilles, in his disguise as a woman. The house at Tarrant Hinton (Dorset) has produced enough wall-paintings to show that there was at least one depicting a large figure scene. However, apart from suggestions that Narcissus (whose fate is described by Ovid in the third book of his *Metamorphoses*) and Perseus (in the fourth and fifth books of the same) are represented, there is not enough detail to establish who or what is going on. On the other hand a fragmentary fourth-century wall-painting from Brantingham (Yorks), depicting a full-frontal image of a woman's face, is more likely to be an important member of the family rather than a goddess or imperial family member as has been suggested.

Most of the mosaics or wall-paintings discussed here were high-quality. However, extant mosaics show that inferior mosaicists also operated. They presumably charged less and catered for a less sophisticated, but socially ambitious, market. The floor depicting

Venus and circus scenes from Rudston (North Humberside) is a good example of one laid by a mosaicist aware of classical mythology but with little appreciation of the iconography. It shows a pigeon-chested Venus with flowing locks confronting a mermaid or a merman. A mirror and a golden apple makes it certain Venus is meant. Complete with extravagant rear quarters, a vulva, and spindly legs the figure is hard to defend on the grounds that it reflects regional traditions of iconography. A floor from Croughton (Oxon) had Bellerophon and the Chimaera as its central scene but a catastrophic error by the mosaicist meant that the central scene was too large for its hexagonal zone. Roughly one-third of the inner circular border was therefore omitted. It suggests the main floor was laid in situ while the central panel was prefabricated elsewhere and arrived on site too late for the main floor to be altered. It seems remarkable the botch was accepted, but perhaps serves to emphasise that the importance of floor scenes was not necessarily very great even to an owner for whom the job must have represented a significant investment.

Villa mosaics were all *a la carte* creations and were invariably individual to their houses, even if they can be attributed to 'schools'. This is a function of seeking exclusivity within a prevailing fashion, making it likely that the mosaics were primarily an expression of personal tastes. Mithraea, for example, are readily identifiable in their architecture and consistent presentation of the god and his associates, regardless of whether found in London or Housesteads. But, Mithras offered many of the same spiritual prospects as those attributed to the worship of Bacchus, Faunus, and Orpheus. If the villa mosaics acted as settings for the practice of cults, then surely there would be more consistency and a broader geographical spread. If the purpose of the Orphic floors was to provide a setting for Orphic ritual then we might expect very similar rooms, and more than one Littlecote triconch hall (**61, 68, plate 13**). If the primary purpose was to own the biggest, best-laid, most innovative and exclusive Orphic floor then we would expect exactly what we do find. The floors are usually in the most prominent rooms in the house, often those identified as dining-rooms, and this suggests a combination of display, recreation, and eating and drinking. The mosaics are much more likely to have reflected in the first place the wealth of the people who commissioned them, and in the second the literary and religious background which will have characterized their education. From this they chose themes and imagery almost as a matter of course, mixing and matching as the mood or fancy took them.

Quite apart from their fittings villas were also where architects and builders were able to experiment. The description by Sidonius of the villa of his friend Consentius as a place of symmetrical architecture with colonnades, baths, entrance and parkland is a vivid image of the villa as a rural palace which dominated the environment but was also integral to it. Woodchester is not the only major villa to have had a procession of approximately symmetrical courtyards, recalling Sidonius' words. Sidonius also expressed his admiration for the architect of the bath-house in his villa at *Avitacum*. Here windows had been designed to draw the eyes of visitors up to the 'cunningly-wrought coffered ceiling'.

Occasionally, collapsed sections of walls give us an idea of what these buildings might have looked at from outside, even when the ground plan appears simple and unprepossessing. At Meonstoke (Hants) an aisled building was extended at one end, requiring a new east facade (**67**). This was created out of brick by an artisan who clearly

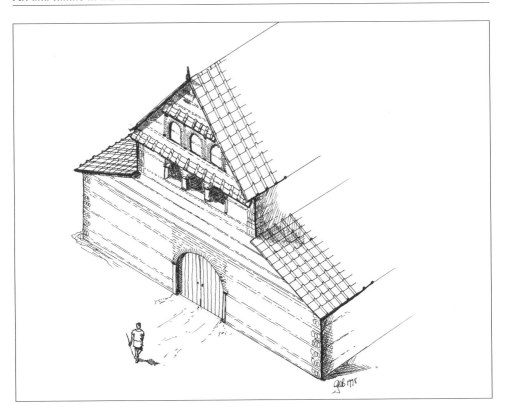

67   *Facade of the fourth-century aisled building at Meonstoke (Hants). The exceptional instance of the survival of a collapsed section of the facade (now on display at the British Museum) has allowed an unusual level of confidence in reconstructing the building's original appearance.*

had considerable experience and a genuine sense of inventive design. He used various forms and colours of bricks to produce two elegant rows of three round-arched windows, one above the other. Subsequently these were blocked up and only survive because the facade collapsed later and the house was abandoned. Decorating architecture in the form of painted plaster, coloured stonework and carving is known from the rest of the Empire to be especially characteristic of the Roman world. It was therefore probably far more common in Britain than the surviving remains of Roman buildings sometimes suggests, though pieces of columns, balusters and other stonework are not unusual finds from the villas of the Cotswolds where stone is plentiful and easy to carve (**59**). At Redlands Farm, Stanwick (Northants) a fallen facade shows how even a small and very modest house had been built by a craftsman who, despite failing to provide adequate foundations, produced skilfully-executed herringbone stonework (**37**).

At fourth-century Littlecote the main house had changed little from its second-century form, resembling the winged-corridor villa created at Bignor a century later, though embellished with towers. But an outbuilding was dramatically converted into a 'triconch' hall. Apart from the Orphic floor within, it resembles early churches in the East, though

LITTLECOTE   **Triconch hall**

68   *Reconstruction drawing of the triconch hall at Littlecote (Wilts). Fourth century.*

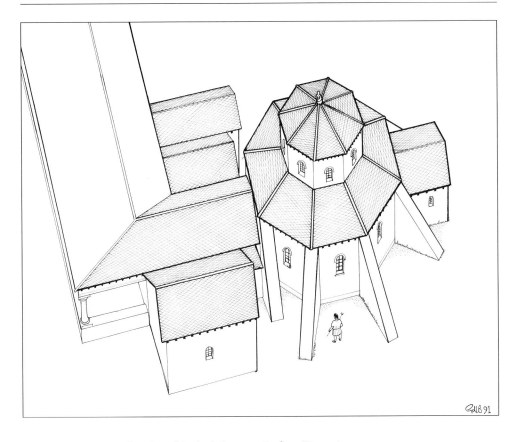

69   Reconstruction drawing of the bath-house at Lufton (Devon).

the height of its walls, roofing and the existence of a tower are all hypothetical (**68**). A cult function, which has been proposed, is certainly not identifiable in the archaeological record. What matters is the nature of the new building, its parallels in the East and the imagination which built it.

At Lufton (Devon) a very ordinary house was augmented by an octagonal bath-suite with a central lantern. Designed by someone who misunderstood the structural implications it was later propped up with buttresses (**69**). A similar experiment at Holcombe (Devon) was sounder. What is particularly interesting is that the Lufton concept had already been tried unsuccessfully in the temple of Apollo at Nettleton. It would also reappear in a more successful execution of the same concept in the sixth-century church of St Vitale in Ravenna. Here the use of internal arches and external buttresses as part of the original design made it viable and it is therefore extant. In none of the Romano-British cases can we trace the architectural heritage of the individual buildings. They may have been constructed to paper designs commissioned by owners who had travelled in the East and taken a fancy to a design, the structural requirements of which neither they, nor their hapless builders, understood. Or, they may represent genuine innovation, their problems illustrating the empirical nature of ancient architecture.

The overwhelming feature of art and architecture in fourth-century Roman Britain is that it seems to have been essentially private. Few of the new fourth-century temples have produced traces of the ostentation and architectural innovation so evident at the villas. The flamboyant temple and bath complex at Bath was maintained on a make-and-do basis by the mid-fourth century. The spring cover building was propped up with architectural buttresses (**plate 27**), while the imaginative octagonal temple at Nettleton had been in ruins since about 330.

In the military zones imposing forts belonged to history. The forts of Hadrian's Wall were degenerating into ramshackle compounds. Resources, if available, were spent on accommodation for the commandant, for example at South Shields. To the west the gates of Housesteads were propped up with timber. In the towns defences were reinforced with whatever stone lay to hand while public buildings were unmaintained. There is no indication of any public or military architectural innovation, or imagination, in Romano-British towns during the fourth century. Most new urban buildings were houses and, if there were urban mosaic schools, urban houses seem barely to have benefited. Luxury, ostentation, and indulgence had become a largely private affair, enjoyed by the Romano-British upper-classes. They defined themselves as part of the classical world and this is how they are manifested in the archaeological record.

8 Conspiracies and reconstruction

From the late second century to the early fifth Britain provided the resources for a series of usurpers. Their ambitions ranged from regional autonomy to making a bid for the Empire but each reflected Britain's potential to act as a military powerbase and the increasing economic and social regionalization of the Empire. The willingness to contribute to insurrections might be seen as proof of Britain's superficial romanization. But the evidence suggests that amongst her elite exactly the opposite was true. Their prestige possessions and expressions of status were classical in form, however gauche, so the idea that there remained a dream amongst the elite of returning to tribal 'roots' and the 'scurf' of a Celtic language would be absurd.

The isolation from mainstream classical culture was perhaps also borne out of economic self-sufficiency. Fantasies of independence may have characterized some of the rebellions but it is just as possible that they were driven by the economic interests of a provincial upper-class. The need to feel part of the classical world was balanced by a reluctance to see wealth being drained by the ceaseless demand from the Empire for men, materials, and money. In the early fourth century few places in the western Empire were safer than Britain. The investment in villas and endowments of new pagan temples fit a picture of an elite community which believed itself secure. But during the second half of the fourth century there was a distinct decline in villa development. The kind of decay which is so visible in the towns over the preceding century (**32, 70**), began to affect the countryside. Unfortunately for Britain her involvement in insurrections made her increasingly a place the Empire could do without. As her own insecurity grew the protection offered by rebellions often seemed the only chance of stability and she veered between participation in revolts and bleating for help from the Empire.

In 348 Constantius II and Constans reformed the silver-washed bronze coinage, producing issues similar to the *follis* of Diocletian. Like the latter they are also rare in Britain, either because of limited supplies or because their higher value meant they were looked after (**71**). Magnentius issued coins which emulated them in size but after his defeat they were probably demonetized and called in. This would explain their scarcity and the outburst of Romano-British copying of some of the reformed coins of Constantius II and Constans. These coins, bearing the fallen horseman reverse with the legend *Fel[icium] Temp[orum] Reparatio* ('The restoration of happy times!'), are found in enormous numbers and are of hugely varying quality. The official versions had been issued before Magnentius, but were revived after 353 perhaps because they seemed appropriate. The extensive copying shows us that cash-based trading must have still been going on in Britain. The copies are unlikely to have been manufactured after the accession of Valentinian I in 364.

70   *The theatre at* Verulamium *(St Albans) looking north. By the fourth century the theatre had become a public rubbish dump.*

In the 350s Constantius II was preoccupied with governing an Empire on his own. In 355 he had to place his cousin Julian in command of Gaul and the north-west frontier which relied on produce from Britain. According to the historian Libanius, Julian became concerned about corruption in Britain and sent financial officers to the island to see where the money was going. Money set aside to pay for the army and its campaigns was disappearing into the pockets of the officers. The commandant's extravagant house at South Shields may have been paid for by a similar fraud. Julian dealt with the corruption, though we are not told how, and then turned his attention to the transport of produce across the North Sea to the Rhine. Barbarians had blockaded the Rhine, preventing freight movement to the Rhine troops. Instead, food from Britain was landed on the Gaulish coast and carried on carts across country. Julian's solution was either to clear out barbarians or negotiate peace terms as appropriate, and build more cargo ships and granaries, all largely achieved by 359.

Building new transports did not guarantee Britain's safety. Marginalised from the main effects of barbarian incursions Britain had grown fat. In 360 the Scots and Picts conspired to cause havoc in Britain's frontier region. News reached Julian in Gaul but, unlike Constans in 343, he was anxious not to leave Gaul which was under threat from the Alamanni. Instead he sent Lupicinus, 'commander of the armed forces', who crossed in midwinter from Boulogne to Richborough with frontier forces, and headed for London to make his base. But, Lupicinus had also been sent to keep him out of the way during an imperial power struggle. An imperial agent was despatched to prevent anyone crossing to

140

71   *Top. Bronze coin of Constantius II (struck c. 348-54) with the 'falling horseman' reverse and
the legend* Fel Temp Reparatio *('The restoration of happy times'). This issue was
extensively copied in Britain. Mint of Constantinople. Diameter 25mm.
Bottom. As above, but with Constantius bearing the labarum (Christian banner) on the
reverse. Mint of Thessalonica. Diameter 21mm.*

Britain to keep Lupicinus informed about events on the continent. Julian had been
declared supreme emperor by his troops when they rejected Constantius' order that they
serve in a Persian War. In the ensuing revolt Constantius died in 361 and Julian ruled alone
until his own death in 363. The impact of Julian's pagan restoration has already been
discussed (see Chapter 6), and he is likely to have enjoyed support in Britain. Meanwhile,
Lupicinus had returned to the continent. Unfortunately, nothing more is known about his
activities in Britain.

Valentinian I became emperor in 364, following Julian's death in 363 and the brief reign
of Jovian. He appointed his brother Valens to rule the East while he took care of the West.
Division of the Empire this time was permanent. Ammianus also describes a number of
barbarian troubles at this point in his text, including the information that the Picts,
Saxons, Scots, and Attacotti were subjecting the Britons to 'uninterrupted hardships'
(*aerumnis continuis*), implying an ongoing state of affairs rather than new problems. The
most satisfactory explanation is that Ammianus is describing the general problems which
afflicted the reign rather than new incursions.

In 367, while travelling to confront the Alamanni, Valentinian heard that a catastrophe had struck Britain. Understanding what happened depends on how Ammianus is read. By acting independently the barbarian tribes traditionally failed to fulfil the potential effect of their raids. In 367 this changed, perhaps thanks to the emergence of more effective leadership helped by corrupt imperial frontier troops. Ammianus called the new development a 'barbarian conspiracy' which reduced Britain to a state of 'extreme need', which may or may not mean that the disorder caused a famine. The main participants were the Picts, made up of the Dicalydones (Caledonians) and Verturiones, and the Scots in Britain, while the Franks and Saxons ravaged Gaul.

Nectaridus, 'count of the maritime area' (possibly another name for the count of the Saxon Shore), was killed. The Duke, Fullofaudes, was ambushed and captured. Ammianus describes bands of barbarians roaming across Britain accumulating loot, prisoners, and cattle. This colourful image of mass destruction is unlikely to be accurate. Medieval armies laying waste tended to have marked localized effects along their routes across the countryside. During the Hundred Years' War in France the presence of an army could cause a colossal increase in food prices in one place, while as little as twenty or thirty miles away prices remained almost normal. The effects of a barbarian conspiracy in Roman Britain were probably catastrophic for a few at most. There is no evidence of widespread damage even as burnt layers in towns, so convincingly identified for the much earlier Boudican Revolt at Colchester, London, and Verulamium.

The upshot was probably more to create a climate of crisis, which provided good copy for historians, promoted hysteria, and disrupted the economy. There is a difference between actual mass destruction, and a fear of mass destruction, but this will not have affected a desire to deal with the threat. There may have been more pressing problems in Britain requiring attention, depending on whether the 'extreme need' to which Britain had been reduced means a shortage of food. If so, the most dangerous areas will have been the army in Britain, and then the towns, which would have been the first to experience the shortage. An initial response came in the form of sending over Severus, commander of the imperial household troops. He was soon recalled though no reason is given by Ammianus. Then someone called Jovinus was despatched and, depending on how the text is read, either he or someone else was allowed to come back by Valentinian in order to raise a proper army to recover Britain.

Theodosius, who enjoyed a considerable military reputation, was subsequently chosen to lead the new force to Britain. He sailed to Richborough and waited for his main forces of Batavians, Herulians, Jovians and Victores to catch up. Then he marched to London where he dispersed his troops who, being fresh and presumably largely mounted, apprehended bands of barbarians slowed down by crates of booty. If true, it would follow that the barbarians were probably largely confined to following lines of communication. Ammianus does not refer to any other parts of Britain, or cities by name, which suggests that Theodosius was mainly concerned with the south-east, the area thought to correspond to the boundaries of the province of *Maxima Caesariensis*.

Recaptured loot was returned to its owners, and prisoners were released. Theodosius withdrew to London, received the usual ovation, and then set about repairing the province. By making the most of intelligence gathering he realised that the barbarians

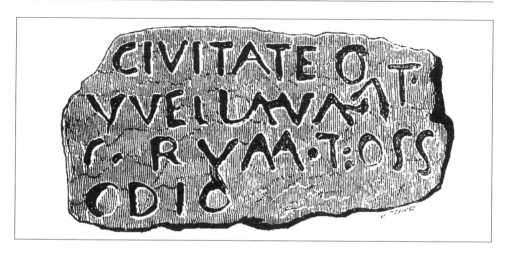

72   *Civitas building stone first recorded near milecastle 55 on Hadrian's Wall, between the forts of*
Birdoswald and Castlesteads. It records work under the command of Tossodio of the
Catuvellauni. Probably fourth century. Diameter 457mm. (RIB 1962; after Mossman.)

were too coordinated to be defeated by a single battle; in any case the level of provincial
disruption was evident from the large numbers of army deserters. Theodosius recalled
them by issuing pardons. He then asked that Civilis, an irritable, but just, man, be installed
as Vicar of the Britons, assisted by Dulcitius as Duke.

London was renamed *Augusta* around this time. Ammianus is not clear about whether
the renaming happened before, during, or after the events of 367. *Augusta* was not an
uncommon name for a Roman city, usually in the form applied, for example, to Turin. It
was known as *Augusta Taurinorum*, 'Augusta of the Turinians'. London's name in such a
form is otherwise untestified and no longer had a mint, depriving us of corroboration
from the mint-marks.

Theodosius also 'restored' (*restituit*) towns and forts. With no identifiable 367 'level' in
the archaeology of towns and forts it is difficult to know what he did. Rebuilding could
have been made by necessary thanks to normal deterioration. The addition of bastions to
London's walls are usually attributed to post-367 reconstruction, but this is only an
approximation. A new ditch added to the city's defences can only be attributed to between
350 and 375. Elsewhere, for example Great Casterton, the late bastions are now known to
have been added before 367, while at other towns such as Leicester were never built. Post-
367 coins and rebuilding are found on Hadrian's Wall and its hinterland which at the very
least shows that the 'conspiracy' did not lead to the Wall's abandonment, even if occupation
in the late fourth century and beyond was less overtly military. At Birdoswald a community,
perhaps the descendants of the garrison, survived long into the fifth century. Watchtowers
on Anglesey, commanding extensive views of the Irish Sea, seem to have been late-fourth-
century additions to western defences while the fort at Caernarvon was rebuilt.

The civitas building stones from Hadrian's Wall may belong to this period but could
date to any time in the fourth century (**72**). On the north-east coast a series of signal

73   *Inscription from the tower at Ravenscar, near Scarborough, recording work by Justinianus the* praepositus *and Vindicianus the* magister *(?). Diameter 558mm. (RIB 721.)*

towers could also be from this period. At Ravenscar a tantalizingly uninformative and semi-literate inscription records the work as having been done by a *praepositus* (commander), called Justinianus, and Vindicianus, a superintendent of works (**73**). The latter office depends on accepting *magister* as the correct reading of the meaningless *masbier*. Presumably the mason was illiterate but had apparently copied the words from a draft by someone who was not; if so, it seems odd that the latter should have tolerated such a garbled inscription at a time when to bother to make one at all was remarkable. It goes on to say that the tower and surrounding compound were built from ground-level by these men.

‘Restoration’ thus may have meant no more than restoring systems and government. Ammianus describes the restoration by Theodosius of a British province, now named ‘Valentia’ to commemorate the event occurring under Valentinian I. The perceived scholarly problem is whether this means the renaming of one of the existing four provinces, or a new province which was a territorial accretion to Roman Britain. It is plain from Ammianus that the province was ‘recovered’, ‘restored’, and, ‘thereafter’ named Valentia. However, the *Notitia* appears to list five provinces of Britain. *Valentia* is the second named, following *Maxima Caesariensis*. The most convincing explanation which has been proposed is that, because the *Notitia* was compiled at different times, a mistake crept in and *nunc* was omitted. Restored, the text reads *Maxima Caesariensis nunc Valentia* (‘*Maxima Caesariensis*, now [named] *Valentia*’). On the assumption that *Maxima* was the south-east with London as its capital, this fits the description of events by Ammianus, in particular the lack of any description of fighting outside the London area.

Theodosius was also faced by treacherous frontier scouts called the Areani (or Arcani). Established under Constans to patrol border country and spy on barbarians they had,

74   *Bronze coin of Magnus Maximus (383-8). The reverse depicts Maximus raising a female figure, symbolizing his claimed recovery of the state. Mint of Arles. Diameter 22mm.*

allegedly, been bribed to tell the barbarians about Roman troop movements. If the barbarians were in a position to bribe the Areani they must have had money or booty they could afford to part with, and were confident there was more. Like all troops in history the Areani doubtless believed they were underpaid and overworked. Theodosius is said to have ejected the Areani from their bases. The outpost forts beyond Hadrian's Wall, like High Rochester and Risingham, where they may have been stationed, show no certain signs of occupation in the late fourth century.

Theodosius is, not unnaturally, presented by Ammianus as the returning hero when he was recalled in 369; the Romano-British were 'dancing for joy'. Yet Ammianus also describes other events in Britain which show that his popularity was far from universal. A Pannonian called Valentinus, exiled to Britain because of some unmentioned crime, started to foment opposition to Theodosius. He made overtures to the army and to other exiles. Although Theodosius ran an effective intelligence operation and was able to apprehend Valentinus it is interesting that Britain was still being used as an official dumping ground for would-be trouble-makers.

In 375 Valentinian I died and the Western throne passed to his sons, Gratian and Valentinian II. The latter was too young to be of concern but Gratian proved unpopular with the civilian elite and the army, on whom the Empire relied. Gratian favoured deserters from the Alan barbarian tribe, granting them high status in the army and guaranteeing him instant unpopularity amongst conventional troops, especially those in Britain. In 378 Valens was killed in battle against the Goths. Unable to rule alone Gratian granted the East to Theodosius I, son of the general who had restored Britain a decade before.

Magnus Maximus (74), a Spaniard, was a military commander in Britain who had earned a reputation in successful campaigns against barbarians. To the British garrison he looked a better prospect than Gratian. His popularity led either to his troops proclaiming him emperor, or his own personal declaration of the fact (the sources vary), in the year 383. There ended the direct relevance of Maximus to Britain apart from the fact that much of his army was made up from the British garrison, and that he may have returned briefly to engage the Picts and Scots in 384. Unlike Carausius, Maximus embarked on a continental campaign where he was joined by more and more of Gratian's army. Gratian himself was killed by one of his own officers. Zosimus, writing about a century later, said that the British garrison elected usurpers in a search for leadership when they heard about barbarian incursions on the continent. Maximus may well have gained support on the continent for the same reasons but from the Romano-British perspective it meant that their hero was focused on being a hero somewhere else, leaving them even less protected than they had been. In 388 he was defeated and executed in Italy by Theodosius I who restored Valentinian II in the West.

Magnus Maximus issued coinage from several mints in Gaul and Italy, but none of the issues tells us where Britain fitted into his plans. Unlike Carausius, Maximus made only practical use of coinage and confined his messages to standard themes of military and Roman prowess, and the usual claims of restoration of the state. It has long been claimed, on the possibility that London was renamed *Augusta* around 367, that his gold coins bearing the mint-mark AVG were struck in London. This is possible, but it is as likely that the mint was *Augustodunum* (Autun) in Gaul. However, some of the gold and silver has been found in hoards in Britain so it clearly circulated on the island. The Hoxne hoard of 408 or later included one gold coin and more than a thousand silver pieces of Magnus Maximus showing that, at the time it was buried, either Maximus' coin was considered legitimate or its intrinsic value made it good.

Magnus Maximus makes an appearance in contemporary accounts because of his effect on mainstream events. For Britain the consequences were indirect but they demonstrate that she maintained the potential for participating in rebellion. Maximus used Britain as an exploitable resource, not as an ideological, or actual, base. Carausius, for all his bravado, was a man with essentially parochial ambitions, however extravagantly dressed up. Maximus, nonetheless, seems to have been remembered fondly as a popular hero. In Wales, historical lineages of Dark Age kingships were traced back to a Macsen Wledig who may or may not have been Maximus.

The voluble sixth-century chronicler Gildas castigated Maximus for robbing Britain of her defences and exposing her to barbarian assaults from the Scots and Picts. He relates how the Britons appealed to Rome for assistance which came in the form of a 'legion'. The 'legion' dealt with the barbarians immediately and advised the Romano-British to build a wall to keep them out. The 'wall' must in fact be Hadrian's, and while the reference shows that Gildas is flawed, it is possible Hadrian's Wall was repaired; indeed, the fourth-century civitas building stones found on it may belong to this date. With Magnus Maximus dead all the West was ruled by Valentinian II, who is unlikely to have been preoccupied with Britain's problems and died shortly afterwards in 392. The Western throne was then filled by Eugenius, a puppet emperor installed by a barbarian general called Arbogastes. Eugenius was regarded by the poet Claudian as every much of a tyrant as Maximus. This led to more civil war, ending in victory for Theodosius I in 394.

In Britain finds of official bronze coins dating after 379 are far fewer than those before. This time the shortfall was not made good by prolific copying. Considering that copying had been a standard solution for poor supply since the period of the Gallic Empire coinage must have become less essential in Britain. Of course, existing coinage would remain in use but previous bouts of copying suggest that supply failure was likely to lead to copying after around a decade as normal losses ate into the circulating stock. Official supplies were temporarily resumed after Magnus Maximus but they never reached the heights of forty years before. An oddity is the exceptional quantity of bronze coins dated 395–402 found at the Saxon Shore fort of Richborough, amounting to 45 per cent of the total. One possibility is that this had become the port of entry for coinage but that demand for the issues was so low, thanks to a steep decline in low-value cash transactions and an outright rejection of anything not silver or gold, that they were discarded.

In 395 Theodosius died. The Empire was divided between his sons Arcadius, who took the East, and Honorius in the West (**79**). Honorius was Britain's last legitimate Roman emperor. He was only twelve years old in 395, and real power lay in the hands of the Master of Soldiers, Flavius Stilicho. Stilicho was a Vandal general, already related to Honorius by marriage and eventually to become his father-in-law. Stilicho's contribution to Britain is only described in a panegyric by Claudian of the year 400 which refers to his efforts to protect her from Scots, Picts, and Saxons. A possible link is the invasion described by Gildas which followed the return home of the 'legion' sent after the fall of Maximus in 388. But Gildas is unreliable and Claudian's poem may be no more than a routine trotting out of standard achievements, so there is little point in trying to fabricate a detailed narrative. Claudian also makes a more general comment about the perception of Britain as the home of fierce and terrible people, which suggests that whatever the efforts by the Romano-British *honestiores* to create a polite society the popular impression on the continent was of a deeply-insecure and troublesome island which he called 'wild Britain'.

Stilicho wanted to increase the territories controlled by the Western Empire but was unwilling to deal decisively with the Visigoths. This gave the Visigoths the idea that they might succeed in their territorial ambitions in 401, leading to yet further withdrawals of the British garrison to prop up Stilicho's army in 402. According to Claudian this involved 'the legion that had been left to guard Britain', perhaps the one described by Gildas. Not surprisingly, this sustained reduction of the British garrison led to further attempts at usurpation. The year 402 was also the last in which coinage arrived in any quantity, which makes it unlikely that what remained of the British garrison received regular wages.

Imperial administration was on the retreat. The Western Empire was now ruled from Ravenna while the capital of the Gallic prefecture had been moved from Trier to Arles. In response to the distancing of authority the disaffected British garrison resorted to a succession of ill-starred usurpers, beginning by supplanting the incumbent vicar of the Britons, probably a Gaul called Victorinus, and appointing someone called Marcus emperor. The plan, if there was one, may have been to try and secure Britain's stability by re-establishing a workable Gallic zone ruled by someone of imperial status but it is impossible to say whether this was purely a garrison initiative or more widely supported amongst the civilian elite. Marcus was swiftly despatched and followed by Gratian, possibly a civilian, who went the same way. They may have failed to live up to the garrison's expectations. To replace Gratian a soldier called Constantine was chosen, helped by the symbolism of his name. Constantine III, as he is known, crossed to Gaul immediately taking with him his sons Constans and Julian and his British general

75   Gold solidus *of Constantine III (407-11). The reverse shows the victorious Constantine and
   a legend denoting his assumed membership of the imperial college with Arcadius and
   Honorius. Mint of Trier. Diameter 21mm. (Copyright — The British Museum.)*

Gerontius. His coinage was all struck on the continent and some carry the reverse *Victoria
Auggg* to denote his unsolicited membership of a legitimate college of emperors (**75**).

Constantine attempted to take advantage of the chaos in Gaul, and the ineffectual
imperial government holed up in Ravenna, to establish a new Gallic empire of Britain,
Gaul, and Spain. However, Constantine's troops sacked the provinces they passed through
and barbarians exploited the disorder to launch new raids. By 410 Constantine's regime
was falling apart. Gerontius had revolted in Spain when Constantine expanded his
ambitions to attempt the conquest of Italy; meanwhile, the Britons had thrown out any
imperial officials they could find and sorted out their own defences, which suggests that
Constantine III had never enjoyed wide popular support in Britain. Many years later in
Gaul Ecdicius, a member of the imperial house and friend of Sidonius, used his own means
and those of other 'great men' to raise a 'public army' which confronted Goths much more
successfully than the official forces. This may have been what happened in Britain.

Honorius seized the advantage and ordered his army to engage Constantine III, then
besieged at Arles. Constantine was defeated, and executed. The consequence was merely
to enhance the image that Britain was a problem that the official Empire, plagued by
continental barbarians, could do without. In 410 Honorius is reputed to have severed
Britain from imperial government, instructing the civitas governments to organise their
own defences. The source concerned however is a dubious one and may not even refer to
Britain. But it makes no difference; the Romano-British had already set their own agenda
and the reality is that imperial control had lapsed, never to be resumed.

There is little in the recorded events of the later fourth century which can be easily
linked either to the Romano-British *honestiores* or even archaeology. Only the army makes
frequent appearances but in a rather vague form, with little useful information that would
help pin down which part of the garrison, and from where, participated in which
usurpations. The events of 367 cannot be convincingly tied to archaeology. All we have is
the evidence for a general winding down of most of the bigger villas and the decline of
public investment in towns.

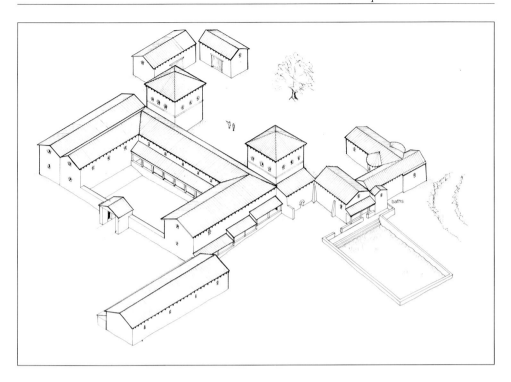

76   *Reconstruction drawing of Gadebridge Park in its mid-fourth-century form. It was demolished and cleared away soon after. (Based on views by Neal, but adapted.)*

The second half of the fourth century certainly marks a downturn in the fortunes of some of the villas. The house at Gadebridge Park (Herts) had existed since the first century, probably marking an estate which had been handed down from the Iron Age. In the early fourth century it had become an elaborate version of the winged-corridor design. By around 360 it had been demolished. Subsequently, farming continued on the site and stockades were built on the site (**76**).

Gadebridge's demise fits the general context of the years after 350 during which it seems some of the *honestiores* found their way of life under threat. Paul's pogrom after Magnentius must have affected a few but there may have been other, more general, problems like disruption to markets and communications in the year 367. An equally plausible explanation is that the owners were bought out. When Pliny the Younger considered buying an adjacent estate to his own, some of the arguments he put forward in favour included being able to use his staff to run both, and to keep only one house in habitable state while the other was only maintained structurally. Gadebridge may just represent the next stage: purchase of the estate by neighbours and then deliberate demolition of the houses to save running costs and prevent unwanted squatters.

More often the villas appear to have decayed naturally, not necessarily involving abandonment, and caused by a lack of maintenance. In these cases the occupants may have been the original owners or their descendants, living in reduced circumstances. At

Middleton Park in South Carolina the family fled during the Civil War, stashing their treasures, only to return in 1865 to find that of the three buildings only one remained habitable, the Union army having burned the other two. Here destruction by an 'internal' force caused the irrevocable alteration of a family's economic and political circumstances. The end of slavery and the decline in demand for rice deprived them of their exceptional income. Although they recovered their valuables they were never able to fund the rebuilding of the two burned houses, which remained in ruins until an earthquake in 1886; instead they occupied the third until after the Second World War. In modern Britain it has been economic and social factors which have led to the demise of many minor stately homes, often linked to the impact of the world wars or ill-starred commercial ventures. The structural and archaeological effects of these events will be familiar to Romano-British archaeologists.

Houses of course had always been in danger of burning down but until the late fourth century when this occurred they were usually repaired or replaced. Now they were usually not. Some examples from the same general area show how varied individual histories might be. Keynsham (Avon) was partially destroyed by a fire of uncertain fourth-century date and involved human remains being abandoned in the debris. The ruins were reoccupied by people who installed crude hearths on top of levelled rubble over the old tessellated floors. At North Wraxall (Wilts) three bodies ended up in the villa well in the late 300s. According to Sidonius, a century later, the marauding Goths in Gaul tried to conceal the number of people they had killed to minimize recriminations. Corpses of victims were dumped in houses, apparently any houses, which were then fired. Other houses near Keynsham, like Brislington and Kings Weston, were fired too and this has been plausibly linked to their proximity to the Severn Estuary and the Bristol Channel, and thus exposure to seaborne raiders.

However, the temple at Brean Down, prominently displayed on a headland projecting into the Bristol Channel, seems to have fallen down as a result of deliberate dismantling and natural decay. The house at Frocester Court, no less accessible to 'seaborne raiders', had a different history in the late fourth century. Here a bath suite was added in the 360s, and the house with its walled garden remained in occupation on into the fifth century. Across Britain in Kent, the house at Lullingstone remained in use into the early fifth century before being quietly abandoned.

The process of collapsing systems in late Roman Britain is very difficult to trace. The demise of the pottery industry is perhaps the least obscure. As such a ubiquitous find pottery marks better than anything else the abundance of manufactured goods in Roman Britain. From the late third century (although output had begun in the first century) the Alice Holt/Farnham grey-ware industry dominated coarse wares in the south, with distribution clearly showing the role the Thames had played in its success. But by the early fifth century it had ceased production. The absence of this fundamental industry must mean that the economic stability which could sustain the infrastructures of manufacture, marketing, and distribution had all disappeared. In the north the Crambeck coarse-ware industry died out at the same time.

Archaeology of late-Roman levels in towns is still at a pioneering stage, and compromised by the destruction of evidence by medieval occupation or early

77 *The south wall of the baths-basilica (exercise hall) at Wroxeter (Salop), showing the entrance to the baths beyond. Extensive excavations in the remains of the hall in the foreground have revealed intensive occupation amongst the ruins right through the late Roman period and beyond into the fifth and sixth centuries.*

archaeologists. But work at Wroxeter has shown that, despite decaying public buildings, towns may have experienced a reprieve as defendable compounds enjoying commercial and social activity well into the fifth century and beyond (**77**), perhaps reflecting the records of defensive self-sufficiency during Constantine III's usurpation. In time archaeology may reveal similar continuity at some villas which has, up to now, gone unnoticed. But, the general cessation of villa life is plain enough in the physical decay of the buildings, not to be confused with the survival of estate and field boundaries. Their former glory emphasises how remarkable conditions had been until that time. Such displays of status are only valid in a system where they constitute recognizable credentials. Many holdings of wealth probably became static and could not be increased because the circumstances which had allowed their accumulation had gone.

The result was the disappearance of evidence for the wealthy Romano-British elite in the form of their extravagant rural homes. The circumstances which had allowed them to express their wealth this way had evaporated and there is very little evidence at all for the commissioning of mosaics or wall-paintings after about the year 390, though the unfinished Thetford jewellery (see Chapter 9) shows that the commissioning and manufacture of luxury goods had not entirely ceased. The *honestiores* now lacked the opportunity to exhibit status and instead they hoarded their possessions. Hoxne and Thetford show that at least a generation or more after the villa luxury trades had declined some people were still in possession of fantastic quantities of gold and silver coin and artefacts and were determined to hold onto them. Legal sanctions against paganism in the late fourth century led to seizures by zealous clerics elsewhere in the Empire, but we do not know if this had much impact in Britain. Further potential for loss came through theft or even through requisitions to pay off threatening tribes. The Romano-British with remaining wealth had now no alternative but to regard their assets as frozen.

9 Treasure hoards and the end

By severing official links with Britain the Roman state ceased to have an obligation to risk allocating troops to a zone which was of marginal significance. One of the few explicit archaeological manifestations of this was the cessation of Roman official coin supply in 402. The Romano-British will not have interpreted the new state of affairs as permanent. The hoards show that, whatever the political and military circumstances, some people had managed to cling on to considerable wealth right up to the end and beyond, in spite of the decay so evident in the towns and the villas. With the collapse of a fluid economy, manifest in the termination of industries like potting and the ending of the taxation system, money was not required to lubricate commercial exchange. This made bronze coinage worthless while gold and silver became the only reliable form in which wealth could be stored.

Hoarding by burial was the standard practical method of protecting valuables in the pre-modern world. Although it increased during periods of uncertainty, hoarding occurred at all times and in all places. Gold and silver provided the best medium for storing a large amount of wealth in a portable form. In the normal course of events hoards were recovered in order to redisplay plate, and pay taxes and other debts. The residue may then have been rehoarded, and perhaps added to, recovered and so on. All that remain are the caches which at some point in the cycle were lost, forgotten about, or whose owners were prevented from recovering them. Individual high-value items normally only enter the archaeological record through casual loss, and for obvious reasons this was (and is) extremely rare. As a result hoards are the most important source of surviving ancient treasure. Although the make-up of a hoard belongs to the time of deposition, the constituent parts may be much older and of varied dates. This is most easily demonstrated in coin hoards. The physical presence in Britain of an individual piece of plate in a hoard is only certain for the time of burial and there is no context in which it can be placed, other than the hoard.

In the Roman world gold and silver coin was in an almost perpetual state of being recycled. It was taken in by the state, melted down, and restruck. The archaeological consequence for Britain was that late gold coin hoards are more likely to be dominated by coins which date from the late fourth or early fifth century because the end of official control shortly afterwards meant they were never withdrawn to pay taxes or other debts. Had the Roman state maintained control then more of these hoards would probably have been recovered. There will have been many more hoards of an earlier date where this happened and thus they do not exist now for us to find.

There is no evidence to link the fourth-century treasure hoards specifically with individual villas of the same period. This also applies to isolated finds like the lanxes from Corbridge and Risley Park (**78, 80**). Thanks to the cessation of coin supply a hoard like

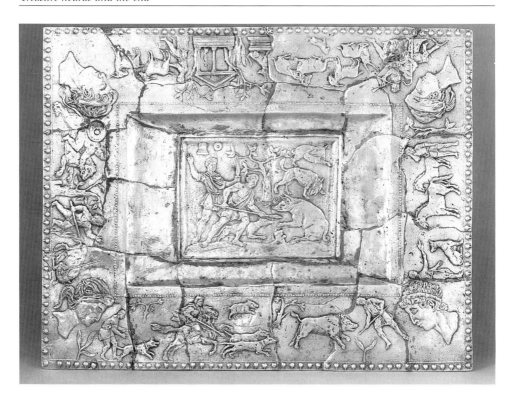

78   *The Risley Park lanx, as restored from a mould taken from reassembled fragments. The scenes are mainly concerned with hunting though the inclusion of a shrine adds a pagan tone. The inscription noting its gift to the church of* Bogium *by Bishop Exuperius is on the underside. Diameter 497mm. (Copyright — The British Museum.)*

Hoxne could, in fact, have been buried up to several decades later than the date of the last coin. The find-spots of the four major modern treasures, Hoxne, Mildenhall, Thetford, and Water Newton, are remarkably close to one another (**1**). However, other recorded material like the Corbridge and Risley Park lanxes, and the Backworth treasure (Northumberland), come from very different areas but they tend to have been found in the eighteenth and nineteenth centuries. That led to instant dispersal, and even melting-down, with the result that they now compare poorly with something like the Hoxne hoard. The fate of the Risley Park silver lanx is the most eloquent example of what could happen. Found probably in the 1700s, it was hacked into pieces and dispersed. Fortunately the process was stopped, the pieces retrieved and then reassembled by some enterprising aesthete. A mould was made from the repaired lanx and the silver melted down, the inherent loss being made good with slugs of identifiably modern silver. The lanx was recast to create a solid copy of the original which has survived to modern times. This extraordinary story only serves to show how precarious a path late-Roman plate has had to tread to reach us. There can be no doubt that the vast majority ceased to exist a very long time ago.

79   *Left. Bronze coin of Arcadius (383-408). Diameter 22mm.*
     Right. Bronze coin of Honorius (393-423). Diameter 19mm.

These, and other isolated finds, show that it is safer to assume such material was originally present in most of the settled areas of Roman Britain and not to attach much significance to the distribution of find-spots. But, frustrating though the lack of direct associations with settlements are, the hoards are in reality normally where we should expect them to be — as far as possible from anywhere looking like an expensive house or temple. The Appleshaw pewter hoard was found close to a house, but this is unusual and its relatively low value will made its security less vital (**55**). Although the Water Newton Christian plate was found within the boundaries of the town the circumstances of its discovery mean that it cannot be associated with a building.

Many of the great villas will have been prominent ruins for centuries (as some still are in Mediterranean countries), attracting attention from peasants and opportunists from time immemorial. The diarist and writer John Evelyn (1620-1706), an enthusiastic coin collector, was keen to advise his readers on useful sources of new material. The situation he describes shows that, were any great hoards buried near Roman structures, they had little chance of surviving to modern times:

> The means of procuring ['medals'] the most authentick and likeliest to be truly antient, is frequently from countrey people, who labour with plow and spade, and such as are employ'd in digging about old banks, mounds, high-ways, foundations and ruins, where happly stations, castramentations have formerly been; where Legions have been quartered, battles been fought, buildings and publick works erected, and the like ...
>
> There is hardly city, town or castle, port, old Roman fosse, causeway or remarkable eminency near them, whether now or antiently standing and appearing in any County of England where medals and coins, Roman, Saxon, Runic, Norman, etc. have not been found, and are daily yet discover'd: Nay, I have been told that in some such likely places, they will give more by the acre for land in purchase, in hope of some lucky chance.
>
> (*Numismata*, 1697, 198-9)

80   *The Corbridge lanx. Found in the Tyne at Corbridge, and probably once part of a hoard. The deities include Apollo, Artemis (Diana), and possibly Leto (mother of Apollo and Artemis) and Asteria Ortygia, all associated with the island of Delos. The island was visited in 363 by Julian II. Diameter 480mm. Engraved by Gerhard Vandes Gucht from a drawing by William Shaftoe.*
(Copyright — The British Museum.)

Perhaps the most remarkable revelation here is that the prospect of loot could elevate seventeenth-century land prices. The tradition was well-established. The *Anglo-Saxon Chronicle* states for the year 418, 'In this year the Romans collected all the treasures which were in Britain and hid some in the earth so that no one afterwards could find them, and some they took with them into Gaul'. This must mean that during the fifth century and later, Roman 'treasure' had been often found and was automatically associated with the violent tale of the end so fondly recounted by chroniclers of the time. But Britain is unusually productive of recorded late-Roman gold and silver hoards compared to other provinces, so the *Chronicle* was probably broadly correct in attributing the practice to the closing years of Roman Britain. The hoards which turn up nowadays tend to do so because they were deeply-buried, or were concealed in areas formerly not ploughed. Only advanced agricultural techniques and metal-detectors have created the circumstances for them to turn up.

156

81   *Silver spoon from the Thetford treasure. Thirty-three spoons were found. This example depicts a triton blowing his horn. Length 68mm.*
(Copyright — The British Museum.)

The Hoxne hoard was not buried before 408. Other treasure hoards, like Mildenhall, lack the unequivocal evidence of coins but are attributed to the same time on the grounds of style and context, though of course this is never absolutely reliable. The Thetford treasure, recovered under dubious circumstances, may have been found with coins of Magnus Maximus which were dispersed into the antiquities market immediately. The circumstantial evidence for the veracity of the rumour is strong. If correct, it provides a *terminus post quem* for Thetford of 388 which corresponds almost precisely with the estimated date based on the style and type of the recorded treasure. None of these problems alter the fact that the material could only have belonged to the *honestiores*, or their descendants. Like fine mosaics the material was exclusive and expensive. Its existence, context aside, demonstrates the presence of people who had exceptional levels of wealth in Britain, even if that presence may only have been fleeting in any one case.

Coin hoards provide the only reasonably accurate method of tracing patterns of hoarding, simply because of the date supplied by the latest coin. However, it is just as obvious that we only have unrecovered hoards to work on. In England coin hoards show a peak during the years of the English Civil War, but there is no geographical correlation between hoards and individual battles and campaigns. A general feeling of insecurity rather than soldiers climbing over the garden fence provokes more people to hoard and the same circumstances will inhibit more people from recovering them, either because the bad times lasted long enough for them to forget where the hoard was or die from disease or old age before they felt they could recover their goods, or because they were killed. Even so, the mere fact of an increase in hoarding will elevate the numbers of unrecovered hoards because a proportion will always remain unrecovered due to natural causes.

Peaks of unrecovered coin hoards thus suggest periods of distress, but not the individual fates which befell their owners. Other hoards like Thetford cannot be fixed to these periods so precisely. But the existence of several which seem to belong to the very late fourth and early fifth centuries is still evidence for heightened insecurity which did not cease soon enough for them to have been recovered. The people who buried the treasure hoards must have planned to recover them. They cannot have been expecting Roman Britain to 'end', any more than hoarders of earlier periods.

Gold and silver plate was widely available in the Roman Empire during the fourth century. Shared styles mean many pieces cannot be attributed to anything other than the most general 'eastern' or 'western' origin. The background was Constantine's extravagant consolidation of his regime, making use of appropriated pagan temple bullion, and the comparative stability of the fourth century especially in the East. Unfortunately, there is little evidence to tell us how individual pieces of plate came into the possession of the hoarder. Gold and silver coin, plates and bars, were handed out by the state to the army, state officials and acolytes on an annual and occasional basis. The Munich Treasure (see Chapter 5) is a good example of imperial plate manufactured to high standards of purity, but there is no equivalent from Britain. The most likely candidate for something similar in Britain is the Mildenhall hoard but many of the other individual pieces like the Corbridge lanx could have been gifts distributed amongst supporters.

The Traprain Law (East Lothian) treasure and the Coleraine (Ballinrees) hoard were recovered from Scotland and Ireland respectively, both outside the Empire. The Traprain Law material was largely broken, bent or otherwise damaged (known as *Hacksilber*), and was plainly on its way to the melting pot. The date of burial has been estimated at the early fifth century. The Coleraine hoard, dated to 410 or later thanks to the inclusion of coins, also contained *Hacksilber*, and a number of silver ingots apparently of Roman manufacture. These groups must either owe their origin to loot, bounty, or protection money. Whatever their fate the silver is likely to have come from the house of the wealthy, probably in Britain or Gaul (**82**).

The crucial difference between Traprain and Coleraine, and other hoards, is that the former had a one-way ticket out of the Roman Empire. The contents were not going to be recovered by the original owners. The unrelated nature of much of the material, and its damaged state, suggests it was gathered from a number of different sources and was only valued for its bullion content. It is extremely unlikely that the contents were willingly relinquished, and although possibly stolen, it is as likely the goods had been requisitioned forcibly, by such officials as existed in the early fifth century, for the sake of paying protection money to barbarians. This would explain why the material had been divided into units corresponding to Roman weights. The artistic merit of the silver flagons from the Traprain treasure was of no interest to whoever buried them. The more conventional hoards like Mildenhall and Hoxne were in a different context. Instead of being hoarded because the onset of a barbarian invasion was feared, they may have been buried to protect them from the requisition agents of whatever was left of provincial government.

Amongst the 15,000-odd gold and silver coins from Hoxne were two *siliquae* of Constantine III which show that the hoard was not buried before 408. So it belongs to the very end of the official period of Roman rule but certainly not outside the period of romanized settlement in Britain. Although the earliest coin in the hoard is one of Constantine II, most of the others belong to the period 358-408. This means that the

82 *Fragment of a silver flagon found amongst the Traprain treasure. The scene is identified as the moment when Odysseus' identity was uncovered by his household, but this was clearly of no interest to whoever cut the silver up. Height 150mm. (After Curle.)*

hoard could have been put together in a short space of time from circulating coin in the first few years of the fifth century, a theory supported by the worn state of the Constantine II piece. Most of the coins are unlikely to have been acquired before the last few years of the fourth century. They include examples struck in Antioch in the East which incidentally shows how widely bullion circulated.

Many of the Hoxne silver coins had been subjected to 'clipping', a phenomenon associated with non-availability of new silver and the production of forgeries from the clippings to maintain some sort of coin supply (**83**). Several hundred Hoxne silver coins are believed to have been such forgeries and a number were struck from the same dies as forgeries in a hoard found at Whitewell (Leics). Silver coins seem to have been favoured in Britain, perhaps encouraging clipping and forging. In the rest of the Empire clipping, and fourth- or fifth-century coin hoards containing high proportions of silver, are very unusual. Analysis of hoards has shown that clipping began around the reign of

83   *Silver* siliquae
Left. Full-size siliqua *of Constantius II (struck c. 345-8). Mint of Arles. Diameter 18mm.*
Right. 'Clipped siliqua' *of Julian II (360-3), trimmed for its bullion in the years after 410.*
Diameter 14mm.

Constantine III or later, which fits neatly with Hoxne. Since 317 clipping had been a capital offence. The proliferation of the habit in Britain in the fifth century was probably partly due to the breakdown in law and order. Hoxne and other hoards show that clipped siliquae were still hoarded for their value though there was probably a difference between coinage accumulated long-term for savings and coinage extracted in the short-term from circulating currency. Clipped pieces will have normally been less popular for savings. The clipped coins in the Hoxne hoard were probably taken from circulating coinage in the weeks or months prior to burial.

The preference for silver in Britain may have been traditional and might explain Carausius' enthusiasm a century earlier for producing pure silver coinage. Official supplies of coinage had dried up by the first few years of the fifth century. The coins at Hoxne would not have been drawn into coinage used to pay taxes, thanks to the collapse in official administration. With the only additions perhaps being forgeries of older issues it is thus obviously possible that we may be looking at the hoarding of material which was several decades old when it was buried. The clearest instance of this is the exceptional hoard of gold and silver coins found at Patching (West Sussex) in 1996. Although the gold coins provide a *terminus post quem* of 465 (for a coin of Libius Severus), many of the silver coins were struck between 337 and 411.

In addition to the coins Hoxne contained five silver bowls, four silver pepper-pots (items of the most extraordinary rarity), two silver vases, silver toilet utensils, a silver vase handle, 78 spoons and 20 ladles of different types, and several pieces of gold jewellery (**plates 20-24**). Some pieces were inscribed, and those with any religious content are all Christian. None of the individual items was of any significant size, apart from the fact that most of the spoons can be divided up into different matching sets. It is not clear if this was a body of material drawn from a single household or an accumulation, perhaps by a third party. However, the silver tigress is a handle which has been detached from a silver vase (**plate 23**). That the vase and the other handle were missing from the meticulously-excavated hoard makes it clear that they were buried or stored elsewhere, had already been requisitioned for bounty payments by the state, or the treasure had been stolen. The latter is unlikely because the conservators noted the complete lack of any trace of forcible detachment and the goods had been carefully placed into small containers which were packed into a locked wooden chest. A perfectly feasible scenario is the swift stashing of all small bullion items prior to a requisition party's arrival. Large, unconcealable, goods were sacrificed in the knowledge that substantial wealth had been secured in the hoard. It would make perfect sense to split up one's wealth to prevent total loss.

However, the size of the hoard, and the detached handle, may be evidence for an accumulation of requisitions buried in transit rather than a single private collection. The different spoon sets are compatible with either interpretation. Several names are inscribed on the spoons, with Aurelius Ursicinus making ten appearances, and a number of Christian symbols such as the Chi-Rho, and even the exhortation *Vivas in Deo*, 'May you live in God!'. Although other names appear, for example Peregrinus and Faustinus, or the woman's name Juliana on a gold bracelet, it seems probable that the material came from a wealthy family or several families with Christian sympathies. Nevertheless, reflecting the merging of traditional myth with Christian motifs on the Frampton and Hinton floors, the Hoxne treasure also included conventional iconography. Amongst the four silver pepper pots is one cast as a representation of Hercules fighting a giant called Antaeus (an incident referred to in Ovid's *Metamorphoses*). On some of the spoons dolphins and mythical sea-creatures, found in Bacchic and Christian contexts, are depicted. Another hoard, of 650 *solidi* also dating at least as late as the reign of Constantine III, is reported to have been found nearby at Eye (Suffolk) in or around 1780. This cannot be confirmed as the coins are long since dispersed but it seems increasingly plausible.

With no associated buildings, interpretation of Hoxne is unlikely ever to be conclusive. The *Villa Faustini* is known from the *Antonine Itinerary* to have lain in East Anglia between Colchester and Caistor-by-Norwich. This may have been a small town which had grown up around a particularly wealthy villa estate which had once belonged to someone called Faustinus and is nowadays normally identified with Scole (itself a name of Latin origin) in Norfolk though no association (or villa) has been located by archaeology. Hoxne and Eye lie two and three miles away respectively. The Itinerary belongs to the early third century or later which means that Faustinus himself was long since dead by the time the treasures were concealed. However, the Hoxne hoard was not buried near any known Roman building which suggests a family or household on the move, not out of context for the period or the location, considering the nearby road. Alternatively it represents a decision to bury material at a considerable distance from 'home', wherever that was.

Rattling off the contents of any one hoard gives very little sense of value. Fortunately, the survival of Egyptian papyri and other documentary evidence from the fourth century does provide us with some sort of basis for comparison. An ordinary soldier could expect to be paid up to five *solidi* annually to cover his food while farming estates in Italy might be rented from a major landowner from anywhere between ten and sixty *solidi* per annum. That the Hoxne hoard contained 569 *solidi* in addition to many thousands of silver coins demonstrates the vast wealth that could be held (assuming it was the property of one household, which it may not have been). Hoxne might be an exceptional hoard but that is a modern judgement based on surviving hoards. It is unlikely to have been exceptional at the time.

161

84   Silver spoon from Biddulph (Staffs), bearing the Chi-Rho symbol. The spoon's shape is characteristic of the fourth century. Length 200mm. (Copyright — The British Museum.)

Perhaps one of the most significant factors about the Hoxne hoard is the small size of the components, making the wealth contained within almost infinitely divisible. This contrasts with Mildenhall which can only been dated on style, and the dubious evidence of inscriptions on some of its components. The attribution of its deposition to the 360s is thus only an educated guess, based on estimated dates of manufacture. Parallels for various items stretch from the late third century to the early fifth which at least has the value of suggesting that the plate had been accumulated over several generations. The Greek name Eutherios appears on two of the Mildenhall platters. Associating some of the pieces with a testified official of that name under the reigns of Constantine, Constans, and Julian, either as being deposited in his ownership or by a subsequent owner is a manifestation of the traditional belief that such material is, and therefore was, extraordinary for Roman Britain.

When this view was expressed in 1977, Thetford and Hoxne were yet to be found. Given a revised perception of the more general context, and despite the probability that the Mildenhall plate was manufactured outside Britain, the hoard is just as likely to have belonged to a wealthy Romano-British household. This is even more plausible for other, much smaller, fourth-century hoards like the five silver spoons from Dorchester (Oxon), and the four from Biddulph (Staffs) (**84**) — none of these spoons is individually significant but they probably represent the small plate holdings of modest families in the latter part of the fourth century.

The Christian element at Mildenhall is marginal though items such as the Risley Park lanx show that Christians were content to own and exchange prestige goods which were overtly pagan. The better-preserved Corbridge lanx is even more expressly pagan. It was recovered under vague circumstances from the River Tyne in the 1730s. Depicting a scene involving pagan deities, such as Apollo and Artemis, associated with Delos, it may allude to a visit to the island by the Emperor Julian in 363 (**80**). Other plate found nearby over the following thirty years was destroyed but contemporary accounts refer to a bowl with Chi-Rho symbols. The material had probably all once formed a single hoard exposed by river erosion and dispersed into the water. Interpreting the group is obviously now impossible but the Corbridge lanx could also have belonged to a church. No church of

Roman date is known in the area though the nearby church of St Andrew was in existence by the eighth century and may have replaced a Roman predecessor. Apart from military officials there is no other general context in which to place the hoard. Villas are practically non-existent in the north.

Some of the Thetford hoard consisted of gold jewellery, in various states of completion and including a number of gemstones of much older date. These were in the process of being placed in new, and unused, gold settings (**plates 10, 24**). This is a significant difference from the other major hoards. They were static because their value was fixed in the goods and coin in the state they were in when buried. The Thetford material was in transition. If recovered, the jewellery would have been finished thus elevating its value. If the hoarder was the owner then the finishing of the jewellery would have made it functional. If they were being manufactured for a commission from a third party they would have been sold on, thus converting the labour into money.

If Thetford's suggested date of deposition in the early 400s is correct then some people were still disposed to patronise (and pay for) the manufacture of high-quality goods which were marks of status, and possibly associated with ritual, at a time of upheaval. The hoarder must have expected to recover his goods, so that he could realise their potential value. It seems likely then that the Thetford hoarder had buried his goods on a tactical basis. He may have buried his goods daily, or at least very frequently, whenever he was unable to guard them personally. He will have opted to bury them in a place where they would be easily recovered, perhaps not far from where he worked. The Hoxne and Mildenhall hoards seem to have been more strategic long-term deposits meriting the effort entailed in burying physically-large groups of material in obscure places.

The idiosyncratic designs of the new settings of the Thetford rings, and the lack of any parallels bar a single other ring, also from Norfolk, have led to the conclusion that they were made in Roman Britain (**plate 26**). This is possible but with any such highly-skilled work the individual maker is of more importance than where he or she might have worked. Such craftsmen are likely to have enjoyed mobility over their working lives. Either way the presence of a Faunus cult in late Roman Britain, explicitly referred to on other elements of the hoard, is of exceptional interest, especially in connection with the increasing evidence for an educated pagan elite in Roman Britain. None of the great hoards has even circumstantial association with contemporary buildings and it will remain a mystery how they came to be buried where they were.

The End

During the fourth century the Romano-British elite enjoyed circumstances which allowed them to develop a version of the elitist culture represented across the Empire, even if they failed to impress men like Ausonius and Claudian. This culture was a statement of membership of the classical world, and especially the pagan tradition. They had no desire to withdraw to their tribal roots, even if in practice their colossal land-holdings and accumulation of wealth, coupled with a move away from the towns, revived a degree of local hegemony which resembled that of the pre-Roman tribal warrior aristocracy. Even the pagan revival seems largely to have spurned many Romano-Celtic deities in favour of self-consciously reconstructed Roman paganism. Across their mosaic floors Aeneas, Orpheus, Venus, and other figures from classical myth were paraded. This demonstrates an aspiration to familiarity with all that symbolized Roman tradition. Carausius identified this strain to Romano-British culture and capitalized on it though it is worth recalling Ausonius' caution that surrounding oneself with learning is not the same as being learned. It is a warning not to take this sort of theme too far by building up a picture of esoteric philosopher villa owners living in a world of secret meanings, abstruse allusions, and recondite iconography.

The tendency to secessionism was built on security in the geographical fact of Britain's being an island, its fertility and temperate climate. It also derived from the sustained failure by the legitimate Roman state to preserve the Roman world in its traditional form. Underlying all this of course was economic self-interest, creating a paradox for Romano-British cultural solidarity with the Roman world. The self-contained British garrison provided the practical means for invoking and maintaining rebellion but it is inconceivable to believe that direction and support from the *honestiores* was not fundamental to the ambitions of Carausius and Magnentius. Later usurpers like Marcus and Gratian may even have been drawn from their ranks.

The Romano-British elite enjoyed circumstances which they had every wish to maintain, at all costs. They had no desire to participate in, or contribute to, continental wars against barbarians which represented a total loss to them in terms of money and resources though they happily bleated for help when they wanted it. Some were prepared to invest in rebellions which stood a chance of preserving the status quo. This never actually worked, although Carausius was the most successful in doing so. In the end, Britain's perpetual reluctance to combine cultural solidarity with practical solidarity meant that disposing of her, always possible, became unavoidable. The circumstances which had created wealth for her elite collapsed and she became increasingly dependent on imperial assistance for her safety, compromised in the end by the efforts of Constantine III which finally led to Britain's severance.

This resolved the problem for the Empire but closed the options for Britain. Confronted by detachment from the world, the Romano-British elite found themselves cut off from a lifeline which would systematically destroy all the systems which had supported all the foundations of their provincial classical culture. The *honestiores* who had clung on to their wealth hoarded it in the hope that things would change back. The story of how these people attempted to maintain a semblance of *romanitas* over succeeding decades is a fascinating one. In it the latinity of men such as Gildas and the Patching hoarder, or the imported goods from the Eastern Empire at places like South Cadbury, fit a context in which an educated, classicized aristocracy did its best to sustain a culture which found its highest expression in the great houses of the Romano-British fourth century. Carausius may have failed in his bid for power but he recognized the character of late Roman Britain and the aspirations of its elite. The memory of their Golden Age took a very long time to dwindle.

Chronology

The following dates, sometimes approximate, chart the principal historical events which influenced Britain from the middle of the third century until the beginning of the fifth.

(Rulers in CAPITALS indicate those in actual or nominal control of Britain)

259   Gallic Empire: POSTUMUS seizes control of Britain, Gaul and Germany to create the Gallic Empire

268   Gallic Empire: murder of Postumus, accession of MARIUS followed by his almost immediate murder. Accession of VICTORINUS

270   Accession of AURELIAN
        Gallic Empire: murder of Victorinus, accession of TETRICUS I and his son TETRICUS II

273   Suppression of the Gallic Empire by Aurelian

275   Murder of Aurelian. Accession of TACITUS

276   Death of Tacitus, accession of FLORIANUS, death of Florianus, accession of PROBUS

282   Murder of Probus, accession of CARUS

283   Elevation of Carus' sons CARINUS and NUMERIAN to the rank of Caesar. Death of Carus, accession of CARINUS (West), and NUMERIAN (East) who was murdered the following year

285   Murder of Carinus. Accession of DIOCLETIAN, following the murder of Carinus

286   Appointment of MAXIMIAN by Diocletian to rule the West
        CARAUSIUS, commander of the British fleet, seizes control in Britain and part of northern Gaul

293   Murder of Carausius and accession of ALLECTUS in Britain
Diocletian appoints junior partners (Caesars) to assist him and Maximian: Galerius (East) and CONSTANTIUS I (West). This system is known as the Tetrarchy.

296   Defeat and death of Allectus by the army of Constantius I. Britain passes back under control of MAXIMIAN (Augustus) and CONSTANTIUS I (Caesar)

305   Abdication of Diocletian and Maximian and elevation of CONSTANTIUS I to Augustus in the West, with SEVERUS (Caesar)

306   Proclamation of CONSTANTINE the Great at York following the death of his father, Constantius I, there. This disruption of the Tetrarchic system led to protracted feuds and wars involving Maximian and his son Maxentius

308   Settlement at Carnuntum passes control of the West to LICINIUS (Augustus) and CONSTANTINE I (Caesar), while Galerius (Augustus) and Maximinus (Caesar) held the East. The feuds continued unabated because Maximian and Maxentius, and Maximinus, tried to recapture power

312   Battle of the Milvian Bridge: Constantine defeats Maxentius, using troops partly raised in Britain. The West is now under the exclusive control of CONSTANTINE I, while Licinius controls the East

313   Edict of Milan guarantees total religious toleration

324   Constantine I defeats Licinius

337   Death of Constantine I and accession of his sons: CONSTANTINE II (Britain, Gaul and Spain), Constantius II (the East), and Constans (Italy, Africa and Central Europe)

340   Murder of Constantine II by Constans. Britain passes under control of CONSTANS

343   Constans visits Britain

350   Revolt of MAGNENTIUS in Autun and murder of Constans

353   Suicide of Magnentius following defeats. CONSTANTIUS II becomes ruler of the whole Empire

360   JULIAN, cousin of Constantius II, proclaimed emperor in Gaul

361   Death from fever of Constantius II

363   Death of Julian. Accession of JOVIAN, formerly commander of the imperial guard

364   Death of Jovian. Accession of VALENTINIAN I (West) and his brother Valens (East).

367   Barbarian conspiracy overruns Britain
        GRATIAN appointed joint Augustus in the West with VALENTINIAN I
        Arrival of Count Theodosius in Britain

375   Death of Valentinian I. GRATIAN now rules jointly in the West with his brother VALENTINIAN II

378   Death of Valens. Gratian and Valentinian II rule the whole Empire.

379   Appointment of Theodosius I, son of Count Theodosius, to rule the East.

383   Death of Gratian. MAGNUS MAXIMUS, senior officer in the British garrison, proclaimed emperor in Britain and straightaway invades Gaul.
        Theodosius' son, Arcadius, is made joint emperor in the East.

387   Valentinian II flees from Maximus to the East

388   Magnus Maximus defeated and executed in Italy by THEODOSIUS I

392   Murder of Valentinian II

393   Theodosius' son, HONORIUS, is made joint emperor

395   Death of Theodosius. The Empire is divided between his sons: HONORIUS (West) and Arcadius (East)

407   Proclamation of CONSTANTINE III in Britain. Moves to Gaul

408   Constantine III takes Spain

410   Honorius instructs Britain to look after its own defences

Visiting the Golden Age

Treasures

The principal treasures of fourth-century Roman Britain are on permanent display in the new Romano-British gallery at the British Museum (10–5 Monday to Saturday; 2.30–6 Sunday. Tel: 0171 636 1555). These include the Hoxne, Mildenhall, Thetford, and Water Newton hoards as well as many other outstanding exhibits such as the Thruxton mosaic and the Meonstoke facade.

Villas

1. Bignor (West Sussex) (**2, 43, 44, 45, plates 1, 14, 15**) is the premier accessible fourth-century villa site in Roman Britain. Privately-owned. Admission charge. Access to the north-west and south-east parts of the villa and its celebrated mosaic floors. The cover buildings themselves are now listed structures in their own right. Open 10-5 March and October, 10-6 April to September; closed Mondays except Bank Holidays apart from June to September when the villa is open all week. Six miles (10km) north of Arundel and signposted from the A29 and A285; the winding roads which lead to the villa are very narrow and hazardous in heavy rain.

   OS Ref. SU 987147. Tel: 01798 869500.

2. Brading (Isle of Wight) (**plate 12**). Privately-owned. Admission charge. Access to the villa building and mosaic floors. Open 9.30-5 from April to October daily. South-east of Brading villa close off the A3055.

   OS Ref. SZ 600863. Tel: 01983 406223.

3. Chedworth (Gloucs) (**39, 52, 59, 85, plate 18**). National Trust. Admission charge. Access to the site museum, introductory video, and the various cover buildings in which mosaics and baths are displayed.

   OS Ref. SP 503134. Tel: 01242 890256.

4. Great Witcombe (Gloucs) (**62, plate 17**). English Heritage. Free. Exterior only, accessible at 'any reasonable time'. Mosaics are not accessible. OS Ref. SO 899144 (sheet 163). Signposted from the A417 5 miles (8km) south-east of Gloucester.

5. Lullingstone (Kent) (**66, plate 16**). English Heritage. Admission charge (includes cassette guide). Access to cover building where almost the entire building is on display including the mosaic floor and baths. Open 10-6 from April to October, and 10-4 November to March daily except 24-26 December. Signposted from the A225 in Eynsford. Principal finds, including all the wall-paintings are in The British Museum.

   OS Ref. TQ 529651. Tel: 01322 863467.

85   *Winter personified on a mosaic at Chedworth. Well wrapped-up against the cold, he carries a twig and a dead hare. Fourth century.*

86   *The remains of the house at Lullingstone looking north across the bath-suite. Despite the introduction of expensive new features elsewhere in the house, like a polychrome mosaic, the baths seem to have been allowed to fall into ruin in the fourth century.*

87   The original facing stones on the defences at Cirencester.

6. North Leigh (Oxon). English Heritage. Free. Accessible at 'any reasonable time'. A mosaic in a cover building can be viewed through a window. Two miles (3.2km) north of North Leigh on the A4095. The walk down to the villa is along a steep track.
    OS Ref. SP 397154.

Towns

Little in the way of fourth-century towns can be seen today but the following are of some interest:

1. Caerwent (Gwent) (**25, 31, 53, plate 3**). The spectacular southern city walls of *Venta Silurum* are without doubt the finest and most imposing Roman urban defences left in Britain. Accessible by footpath any reasonable time from the east and west ends of the modern village.

2. Cirencester (Gloucs) (**87**). Part of the late defences, consisting most of the lower courses and foundations only, of *Corinium Dobunnorum* are accessible from a street called Corinium Gate, just off London Road by the eastern bypass. The fragmentary remains of two bastions belong to the fourth century. Corinium Museum in Park Street is also well worth a visit and includes the inscribed base from the Jupiter column of Lucius Septimius (**26**). Open all year except Mondays between October and March and all Sunday mornings.
    Tel: 01285 655611.

88   *Window-frame at the fourth-century townhouse in Colliton Park, Dorchester.*

89   *Pier from the vaulted Great Bath at Bath. The original pier is visible in the centre. When the timber roof was replaced with a vault in the second century the greater weight required vastly stronger piers. By the fourth century the entire complex was beginning to decay.*

90   The remains of the fourth-century Romano-Celtic temple at Maiden Castle (Dorset). See also **plate 6**.

3. Dorchester (Dorset) (**88, plate 19**). The fourth-century townhouse is accessible at Colliton Park by County Hall. The two separate wings are both visible. Look out for the window opening, something which is extremely rare for Roman Britain.

Temples
Temples are probably the most poorly-represented monuments of Roman Britain.

1. Bath (Avon) (**89, plate 27**). The outstandingly well-presented remains of the Roman baths of Bath and the temple precinct of Sulis-Minerva should not be missed at any price. Although the remains and artefacts cover the entire Roman period much modern excavation work has been concerned with understanding the fate of the temple precinct and sacred spring during the fourth century and beyond. Admission charge. Close to the Abbey in central Bath, access from Stall Street.
    Tel: 01225 477774.

2. Lydney (**50**). At Lydney Park the principal Roman structures, including the temple and bath-house of the shrine of Nodens, have been left exposed. However, the site is privately-owned and may only be visited by prior arrangement. Contact the Lydney Estate Office at Lydney, Gloucestershire to enquire about access. East of Aylburton off the A48.
    OS Ref. SO 617025. Tel: 01594 842844.

3. Maiden Castle (**90, plate 6**). The footings of the Romano-Celtic temple at Maiden Castle (Dorset) are visible after a thoroughly energetic walk across the Iron Age hillfort but there is little to see. English Heritage. Access at any reasonable time. Two miles

91   North wall of the Saxon Shore fort at Richborough. The gap marks the site of a gateway. Note the different masonry style to the left. This indicates where two working parties met up.

(3.2km) south of Dorchester off the A354.
  OS Ref. SY 670885.

4. London. The mithraeum by the Walbrook was vandalized during the fourth century. Fortunately for archaeologists the principal contents had already been stashed away and have survived. The temple could not be preserved following excavation but its remains were 'reconstituted' on a streetside site in Queen Victoria Street in the City of London. The nearest tube is at Bank. The finds are displayed at the Museum of London (open daily, except Mondays).
  Tel: 0171 600 1399

Forts

The irony of the Golden Age of Roman Britain is the fact that it became ring-fenced with defensive structures. The remains of the forts of the Saxon Shore are the most prominent, though the bulk of the forts in the north along Hadrian's Wall and elsewhere remained in commission throughout the period.

1. Richborough (Kent) (**10, 91**). The fort was once by the sea but *Portus Rutupiae* is now distinctly land-locked. In spite of this the sea had time to wash away the fort's eastern wall, leaving only the crumbling remains of the other walls to be seen today. The site spans Roman Britain's history and includes a military ditch of Claudian date, associated with the invading force. Subsequently a monumental arch was erected in the centre before it was converted into a fortified look-out tower. The fort of the Saxon Shore was then built around it towards the end of the third century and is described in the *Notitia Dignitatum* as

the base of the II Legion *Augusta*. The site is signposted from the A257 to the west of Sandwich. English Heritage. Open 10-6 (or dusk if earlier) from late March to the end of October (call for exact dates).

    OS Ref. TR 324602. Tel: 01304 612013

2. Portchester (Hants) (**10, 12, plate 2**). This is the finest of all the forts of the Saxon Shore and remains immediately beside the sea. Apart from the fortifications though there is nothing else Roman to see. Its prime location on the south coast made it an inevitable choice as the site for a Norman Castle which is still perhaps the most prominent feature. The crenellations on the walls are of medieval date. Signposted off the A27 just west of Portsmouth. English Heritage. Admission charge. Open all year round from 10, closes at 4 in the winter.

    OS Ref. SU 625046. Tel: 01705 378921

3. Pevensey Castle (W. Sussex) (**10, 11**). Like Portchester Pevensey was also reused by the Normans. Unlike Portchester its straggling oval plan is not immediately an obvious Roman site and, as at Richborough, it is now land-locked. But elements of the walls show striking Roman brick work and the west gate bastions are the best-preserved remains of any gate at a Saxon Shore fort. Off the A259 in Pevensey. English Heritage. Admission charge. Open all year round from 10, closes at 4 in the winter.

    OS Ref. TQ 645048. Tel: 01323 762604

4. South Shields (Tyne & Wear). Although the fort at South Shields was built in the second century and there was almost certainly a fort here before that, this is one of the few places in the northern frontier where active archaeology is going on at the moment. The remains of the fourth-century commandant's house and the late barracks are all currently being exposed. The site is close to the river Tyne as befitted its fourth-century garrison of Tigris boatmen and can be easily reached on foot from central South Shields, or by car. Open all year round except Sundays (open on summer Sunday afternoons) and Mondays. Free. There is a first-class museum.

    OS Ref. NZ 365679 (A-Z ref. p. 35 E5). Tel: 0191 454 4093

5. Birdoswald (Cumbria). Birdoswald was one of the original forts on Hadrian's Wall but owing to the site of a farm on the fort platform it escaped in-depth nineteenth-century archaeology. Recent work here has revealed what may have happened as the Roman military system crumbled during the fourth and early-fifth centuries. The granaries were reused as halls, perhaps the headquarters of chieftain-like leaders, and are on public display. English Heritage. Open from Easter to the end of October only. Admission charge. A little under 3 miles (5km) west of Greenhead, signposted from the B6318.

    OS Ref. NY 615663. Tel: 01697 747602

Sources

Texts

Latin sources for the period referred to in this book, together with those from earlier and later times, may be found usually in the Loeb Classical Library. S. Ireland, *Roman Britain. A Sourcebook* is an invaluable resource for texts in translation but omits material unrelated directly to Britain, for example Ausonius and Sidonius who feature prominently in this book. Other useful material may be found in N. Lewis and M. Reinhold, *Roman Civilization. Sourcebook II: The Empire* (Harper Torchbooks, 1966). The principal references of major interest are briefly listed below in their most familiar forms.

Chapter 1
Florus
on the value of Britain: I.xlvii.4

Tacitus
on the enslavement of the Britons: *Agricola* xxi.2

Chapter 2
Virgil
and the expected one: *Aeneid* ii.283
quoted on the Carausian medallions: *Eclogues* iv.6-7

Chapter 3
Panegyrics, see *XII Panegyrici Latini*, ed., R.A.B. Mynors (Oxford, 1964)
Rome reborn: *XII Panegyrici Latini* viii.19.2
Golden Ages under Diocletian and Maximian: *XII Panegyrici Latini* ix.18.5
Papyrus on legal tender coinage: Oxyrhynchus no.1411, cited by Lewis and Reinhold
Tertullian on Bacchus: *De Corona*, vii.5, and 7

Chapter 4
Augustine
on African pagans: *Letters* L (Loeb no. 16)
on Donatist gluttonous carnality: *Letters* XXIX.11 (Loeb no.10.11)

Ausonius
on town and country: III.i.31-2
on country living: III.i, and X.xx

Pliny the Younger
on his house at *Laurentum*: *Letters* ii.17

Sidonius
on attacks to Auvergne: *Letters* III.ii.2
on factional disputes at Bourges: *Letters* VII.v.1
on the gift of a farm to the church at Clermont-Ferrand: *Letters* III.i.2

Sulpicius Severus
on the council at Rimini, 360: *Sacred History* II.41

Chapter 5
Ausonius
on barges and bailiffs: XVIII.26

Pliny the Younger
on buying up a neighbouring estate: *Letters* III.xix.4
on new tenants: *Letters* X.viii.5
on buying a house for his nurse: *Letters* VI.iii
on the sale of land: *Letters* VII.xi
on bailiffs: *Letters* VI.xxx
Sidonius on the setting of *Avitacum: Letters* II.ii.3
Papyrus of 300 on devaluation: Rylands no. 607, cited by Lewis and Reinhold

Chapter 6
Ammianus Marcellinus
on corrupt requisitions of temple property: XXII.iv.3
on the corrupt bishop of Alexandria: XXII.xi.3-4
on Julian's exploitation of Christian disputes: XXII.v.3

Augustine
on the *Aeneid: Confessions*, i.14

Jerome
on traditional literature: *Letters*, xiv.30
on avoiding drunkenness: *Letters* liv.9-10

Propertius
on drunkenness: I.iii.8ff

Severus Alexander
and his prayers: *Scriptores Historiae Augustae* Sev. Alex. xxix.2

Tertullian
on lust and drunkenness: *De Spectaculis*, x.6

Chapter 7
Ausonius
on Latins and barbarians: III.iii.2–3
on literary rural exile: *A Letter from Symmachus* (see the Loeb edition, vol. I, p.265)
on Silvius Bonus: XIX.107-12

Bible
on house churches: *Acts* ii.46 and *Philemon* 2

Cicero
on sun gods: *On the Nature of the Gods*, III.53ff

Jerome
on the Chimaera: *Letters* cxxv.18, citing Lucretius v.905

Pausanias
on Orpheus: *Description of Greece*, IX.xxx.3

Pliny the Elder
on mosaics: *Natural History*, xxxvi.184ff)
on plate: *Natural History* XXXIII.144, 154-7, 139-46, 155

Pliny the Younger
on his temple of Ceres: *Letters* IX.xxxix
on literary rural exiles: *Letters* vii.25, viii.4

Sidonius
on the architect of the baths at Avitacum: *Letters* II.ii.5
on the decoration of the baths at Avitacum: *Letters* II.ii.6
on chilled drinks at Avitacum: *Letters* II.ii.12
on Consentius' library: *Letters* VIII.iv.1

Suetonius
on Caesar and mosaics: *Divus Julius* xlvi

Varro
on villas: *On Agriculture* III.i.10

Virgil
on the scene alluded to at Lullingstone: *Aeneid* i.50ff
referred to at Otford: *Aeneid* i.313
at Vindolanda: *Aeneid* ix.473

Vitruvius
on mosaics: *On Architecture*, VII.i.4

Chapter 8
Ammianus Marcellinus
on harassment: XXVI.4.5
on the state of Britain: XXVII.8.1
on Valentia: XXVIII.3.7

Claudian
on Eugenius: viii.73
on 400: *On Stilicho's Consulship* ii.247
on Britain: *The Gothic War* viii.73, and xxvi.568
on the legion: xxvi.416

Pliny the Younger
on his neighbouring estate: *Letters* III.xix

Sidonius
on the barbarians' burning of houses: *Letters* III.iii.8
on Ecdicius' private army: *Letters* III.iii.7

Chapter 9
Ausonius
on learning and being learned: XIX.7

Ovid
on Antaeus: *Metamorphoses* ix.184)

Inscriptions (in alphabetical order by place)

The texts of the following inscriptions are the most important ones referred to in the text.

Birdoswald (Hadrian's Wall) (**20**)
[DD]NN DIOC[LETIANO] ET
M[AXIM]IANO INVICTIS AUGG ET
CONSTANTIO ET MAXIMIANO
N N C C SUB V P AUR ARPAGIO PR
PRAETOR QUOD ERAT HUMO COPERT
ET IN LABE CONL ET PRINC ET BAL REST
CURANT FL MARTINO CENT P P C ...
'For our Invincible Lords Augusti, Diocletian and Maximianus, and for the most noble Caesars Constantius and Maximianus [Galerius], under his perfection the governor Aurelius Arpagius, the commanding officer's house, which had become ruinous and covered with earth, was restored and the headquarters building and the baths. The work was carried out by the [....] cohort under the charge of Flavius Martinus, centurion in command.'
Date: 297-305. RIB 1912

Bordeaux (**6**)
DEAE TUTELE BOUDIG
M AUR LUNARIS SE
VIR AUG COL EBOR ET
LIND PROV BRIT INF
ARAM QUAM VOVER
AB EBORACI AVECT
V S L M
PERPETUO ET CORNE
'Marcus Aurelius Lunaris, sevir Augustalis in the colonies of York and Lincoln in the province of Britannia Inferior set up this altar to the goddess Boudiga which he vowed he would do when he set sail from York in the year of the consulships of Perpetuus and Cornelianus.'
date: 237. *Journal of Roman Studies* xi (1921), 102

Combe Down, Monkton Combe (Som) (**41**)
a. PRO SALUTE IMP C(A)ES M AUR
ANTONINI PII FELICIS INVIC
TI AUG NAEVIUS AUG
LIB ADIUT PROCC PRINCI
PIA RUINA OPRESS A SOLO RES
TITUIT
'For the preservation and health of the Emperor Caesar Marcus Aurelius Antoninus Pius Lex Invictus Augustus, Naevius, freedman of the emperor and assistant to the procurators, restored the ruined and tumble-down headquarters from the ground up.'

date: 212-17 or 218-22 (the official names of Caracalla and Elagabalus are normally indistinguishable, as here). RIB 179

b. lead seal
P B R S (with an image of a stag)
'(Seal) of the Province of BRitannia Superior.'
RIB II 2411.37

Cirencester (Gloucs) (**26**)
Face:
I O [M]
L SEPT [...]
V P P B[R PR]
RESTI
CIVIS R[EMUS?]
'To Jupiter Optimus Maximus, his perfection Lucius Septimius [...], governor of Britannia Prima and citizen of Reims, restored [this column].'
Left side:
SEPTIMIUS
RENOVAT
PRIMAE
PROVINCIAE
RECTOR
Back:
[SI]GNUM ET
[E]RECTAM
[P]RISCA RE
[LI]GIONE CO
[L]UMNAM
'Septimius, governor of Prima, restored this statue and column, erected by the ancient cults'.
date: 296-315? RIB 103

Gallows Hill, Carlisle (Cumbria) (**17**)
IMP C M
AUR MAUS
CARAUSIO P F
INVICTO AUG
'[This stone was erected] for the Emperor Caesar Marcus Aurelius Maus(aeus?) Carausius Pius Felix Invictus Augustus.'
date: 286-93. RIB 2291

Kenchester (Hereford and Worcs)
IMP C

MAR AUR
NUMORIAN
O R P C D
'The *ResPublica Civitatis Dobunnorum* [cantonal government of the Dobunni] set this stone up for the Emperor Caesar Marcus Aurelius Numerianus.'
date: 283-4. RIB 2250 (found in the town walls at Kenchester)

London
[PRO SALUTE D N AU]GGGG
[ET NOB CAES]
[DEO MITHRAE ET SOLI] INVICTO
[AB ORIENTE] AD
[OCCID]ENTEM
'For the good of our Lords Augusti and the noble Caesar to the god Mithras and the Invincible Sun from east to west'.
The dating of this stone relies on finding a time when there were four Augusti and when public pagan dedications to the state were still made. The single Caesar is restored in RIB but that line is entirely lost. The only valid period appears to be 307-8 during the reigns of Maximian (second reign), Galerius, Constantine I, and Maxentius.
date: 307-8. RIB 4

Ravenscar, nr Scarborough (E. Yorks) (**73**)
IUSTINIANUS P P
VINDICIANUS
MASBIER TURRE [sic, for MAGISTER?]
M CASTRUM FECIT
A SO(LO)
'The commander Justinianus and the master Vindicianus built this tower and fort from the ground up'.
date: fourth century. RIB 721

Rockbourne (Hants)
IMP CAES
C M Q TROI (sic)
ANO DEC
IO AUG
'[This stone was erected] for the Emperor Caesar Caius Messius Quintus Traianus Decius Augustus'.
date: 249-51. *Journal of Roman Studies* lvi (1966), 219-20

St Hilary (Cornwall) (**24**)
IMP CAES
FLAV VAL
CONSTANTINO

PIO NOB
CAES
DIVI
CONSTANTI
PII FEL
AUG
FILIO

'[This stone was erected] for the Emperor Caesar Flavius Valerius Constantinus Pius, most noble Caesar, son of the divine Constantius Pius Felix Augustus.'

date: 306-7. RIB 2233

York

[NEPTUNO] ET GENIO LOCI
[ET NUMINIB AU]GG L VIDUCIUS
[VIDUCI F PLA]CIDUS DOMO
[CIVITATE] VELIOCAS[S]IUM
[PROV LUGD N]EGOTIATOR
[BRITANN AR]CUM ET IANUAM
[PRO SE ET SUIS DE]D[IT] GRATO ET
SELEUCO COS

'To Neptune, the Genius of the Place, and the Spirits of the Emperors. Lucius Viducius Placidus, son of Viducius, from Veliocasses in the province of Lugdunensis, trader with Britain, donated the arch and gate on behalf of himself and his descendants in the year of the consulships of Gratus and Seleucus.'

The stone is badly damaged but much of the critical detail can be restored from an altar dedicated by the same man found at the estuary of the Scheldt (ILS 4751, Lactor 4, no. 216)

date: 221. Britannia viii (1977), 430, no. 18

Most of these and other inscriptions are published in:

1. Collingwood, R.G., and Wright, R.P., 1995, *The Roman Inscriptions of Britain. Volume I Inscriptions on Stone* (second edition, with Addenda and Corrigenda by R.S.O. Tomlin), Stroud. Volume III (forthcoming) will cover stone inscriptions found since 1955, otherwise published in individual editions of the *Journal of Roman Studies* (1955-69) and *Britannia* (1970 onwards)

2. Frere, S.S. Tomlin, R.S.O. and others, various years, *The Roman Inscriptions of Britain, Volume II Instrumentum Domesticum*, Stroud (issued in a series of fascicules; lead sealings for instance, may be found in Fascicule 1, RIB 2401-2411)

3. Maxfield, V., and Dobson, B., 1995, Inscriptions of Roman Britain, Lactor no.4 (third edition), London (a selection of Romano-British epigraphic records which includes Vindolanda tablets, diplomas, and stone inscriptions — available from the Lactor Publications Secretary, 5 Normington Close, Leigham Court Road, London SW16 2QS)

Further reading

History and archaeology

The two most solid histories of Roman Britain are Peter Salway's *Roman Britain* (Oxford, 1981), re-emerging in 1993 as *The Oxford Illustrated History of Roman Britain* and Sheppard Frere's *Britannia* (Routledge, 1987, reprinted Pimlico 1991) which still has much to recommend it. Benefiting from more recent discoveries Tim Potter and Catherine Johns' *Roman Britain* (British Museum, 1992) is a more thematic and very well-illustrated review as well as being less biased towards the military. Martin Millett's *The Romanization of Britain* (Cambridge University Press, 1990) is the modern classic exposition of Romano-British society and reflects the development of social and economic studies founded on the use of models and extensive statistical interpretation of archaeological evidence.

For the general background A.H.M. Jones, *Decline of the Ancient World* (1966, and later reprints) is an excellent way to see Roman Britain against a greater context. Paul Johnson's *A History of Christianity* (1976, and later reprints) includes a vivid account of Christianity's violent and schismatic impact on the late Roman world.

Pottery and coins

Pottery of the period is amply summarized by Paul Tyers, *Roman Pottery in Britain* (Batsford 1992, now available through Routledge) but Vivien Swan's *Pottery in Roman Britain* (Shire, 1975 and later reprints) is an admirable synopsis. Archaeologists always seem to have had a curious relationship with coins which have remained the preserve of numismatists. Doubtless this is why there is no convenient archaeologists' handbook to coinage. David R. Sear's *Roman Coins and their Values*, (Seaby, various editions) is an outstanding summary and indispensable one-volume guide which also happens to be the most convenient quick-reference guide to the proliferation of emperors, would-be emperors and other opportunists of the late Empire. If it has any shortcomings it is that it barely deals with contemporary copies which made up so much of the third- and fourth-century Romano-British coin stock. P.J. Casey's *Roman Coinage in Britain* (Shire, 1980 and still widely available) makes this good as well as covering other problems of coins from Roman Britain as does Richard Reece's *Coinage in Roman Britain* (Seaby, 1987).

Carausius and the Saxon Shore

For the Carausian Revolt the only worthwhile account is P. J. Casey's *Carausius and Allectus: the British Usurpers* (Batsford, 1994) though the present author's 'Carausius, Virgil, and the marks RSR and INPCDA' in *Numismatic Chronicle* (1998), explores the literary associations in new detail. For the fourth century, and the fifth-century aftermath, Simon

Esmonde Cleary's *The Ending of Roman Britain* (Batsford, 1989) is a comprehensive account of the history and archaeology but with little emphasis on art and culture. The military background of the Saxon Shore is covered by Stephen Johnson's *The Roman Forts of the Saxon Shore* (Paul Elek, 1976, and Book Club Associates, 1979). Tony Wilmott's exemplary publication of the excavations at Birdoswald (English Heritage, 1997) covers the exciting discoveries of the fate of a second-century frontier fort during the fourth and fifth centuries.

Art and culture

More in-depth studies of art and culture in Roman Britain are to be found in Martin Henig's *The Art of Roman Britain* (1995), and Catherine Johns' *The Jewellery of Roman Britain* (1996). Martin Henig's *Religion in Roman Britain* (Batsford, 1984) is useful background to the complexity of Romano-Celtic beliefs as is Dorothy Watts' *Religion in Late Roman Britain* (Routledge, 1998). Wall-painting is considered by Norman Davey and Roger Ling's *Wall-Painting in Roman Britain* (Society for the Promotion of Roman Studies, Britannia Monograph no. 3, 1982), and mosaics by David S. Neal in *Roman Mosaics in Britain* (ibid., 1981). Peter Johnson's *Romano-British Mosaics* (Shire, 1982) is very usefully illustrated and Anne Rainey's *Mosaics in Roman Britain* (David and Charles, 1973) provides a valuable gazetteer. Roger Ling's paper on Roman mosaics in Britain in *Britannia*, xxviii (1997) brings the subject right up to date with a review of recent work and discoveries. At the time of writing a new corpus is planned by David S. Neal and Steve Cosh (for The British Museum Press).

Villas

For villas in general *The Roman Villa in Britain* (Routledge, 1969), edited by A.L.F. Rivet, despite its age, remains the only comprehensive survey of what became an unfashionable subject in more recent times. The Royal Commission on Historical Monuments' *Iron Age and Romano-British Monuments in the Gloucestershire Cotswolds* (HMSO, 1976) is a thorough and extensively-illustrated of the richest of all villa areas. Keith Branigan's *The Roman Villa in South-West England* (Moonraker, Bradford-on-Avon, 1976) discusses the same area and beyond. John Percival's *The Roman Villa* (Batsford, 1976) places the villa in context. The much more recent survey by J.T. Smith in *Roman Villas* (Routledge, 1997) is a curious work which tries to analyse villas by interpreting the function and status of individual rooms. However, the vast number of villa plans make it an interesting trawl.

Towns

The fate of one specific town in the fourth century is usefully summarized and illustrated by Roger White and Philip Barker in *Wroxeter. Life and Death of a Roman City* (Tempus, 1998), and covers the most important series of excavations in a Romano-British town in recent years.

Treasure

Romano-British treasures are best covered by the individual monographs, for example Kenneth Painter's *The Mildenhall Treasure* (British Museum, 1977), and *The Water Newton*

Early Christian Silver (also British Museum, 1977), Catherine Johns and Tim Potter's *The Thetford Treasure* (British Museum, 1983) and John Kent's and Kenneth Painter's *The Wealth of the Roman World. Gold and Silver AD300-700* (British Museum, 1977) is an amply illustrated catalogue of an exhibition which did much to show how ubiquitous the bullion wealth of the late Roman world was. The definitive publication of the Hoxne treasure is forthcoming.

For up-to-date information on discoveries the best source is *Current Archaeology* (9 Nassington Road, London NW3 2TX). Issue no. 157 (May 1998) includes some superb illustrations of fourth-century mosaics planned for inclusion in the forthcoming Neal and Cosh corpus of Romano-British mosaics.

Index

(dates shown are reigns for rulers and usurpers, lifetime for others where known)